The GOLDEN JUBILEE *of* QUEEN ELIZABETH II *and* TORFAEN

By

W.G. Lloyd

HSW Print
Hackman Print and South Western Printers
Unit 1, Cambrian Industrial Estate
Clydach Vale, Tonypandy, RCT, CF40 2XX

CONTENTS

FOREWORD

One of the more striking aspects of Torfaen is its sheer diversity. At the top of the eastern valley, Blaenavon nestles against hillsides rich in the minerals on which the Industrial Revolution was founded. Coming south, the wooded hillsides of the upper valley give way to the urban landscapes and bustling townscape of Pontypool. Below Pontypool Torfaen opens out on to the Gwent levels down to the modern town of Cwmbran.

These major centres of population, and the many communities which go to make them up, create a huge range of different places, different communities, people, and businesses. And although the idea of the "eastern valley" is longstanding, and provides a unity of identity for all these people and places, the idea of "Torfaen" is still relatively young, as history goes. As a name for the communities and Council of the eastern valley it is not yet 30 years old, even though the name itself has links back to antiquity.

But for all this diversity, there are many threads and themes, which bind and unify.

One of the most important of these is the relationship, which the people and communities throughout Torfaen have with their Monarch. And on Jubilee occasions across two centuries the people of Torfaen have taken the opportunity to celebrate and renew their allegiance, and also to strengthen (and enjoy!) their own togetherness.

It is no surprise that street parties, fetes, and open-air gatherings of every sort have regularly marked Jubilees. People from all walks of life having fun. Laughing, dancing, looking at things, eating – oh, and yes, a little drinking too...

So this book is a celebration not only of those occasions which stand as milestones in the reigns of royalty. It also tells us a great deal about what makes the people and communities of Torfaen what they are – places where communities and people are valued, and relationships and the quality of life matter greatly.

This is a wonderful book, full of history and interest, people and anecdotes. Through it you can share the excitement and the exuberance of those many occasions when Torfaen and its communities have played their part in celebrating the Jubilees. It is a great achievement, and I hope that you will find as much pleasure in it as I have done.

Clive Grace
CHIEF EXECUTIVE
TORFAEN COUNTY BOROUGH COUNCIL

iv

FOREWORD

W.G. Lloyd was undoubtedly the right person to ask to write about this historical landmark and the past Royal associations and celebrations of the communities of Torfaen – he is already a popular author with an impressive bibliography of local history to his name. The author's interest and meticulous research into his subjects is well known and is reflected in the sterling voluntary work that he undertakes for the Torfaen Museum Trust at Pontypool Museum and, in particular, with the collections of the Trust's Dobell-Moseley Library and Archive. Mr. Lloyd is always helpful and informative with all researchers who visit the Museum – ready with advice from years of experience and sound knowledge.

It is so typical that he is to donate the proceeds of this excellent book towards the work of the Torfaen Museum Trust; this is indicative of his dedication to the work of the Trust, his love of the history of Torfaen, and his wish to help to preserve the Valley's heritage. On behalf of the Trust Chair, Executive Board, staff and volunteers, I would like to extend my thanks for his help and generosity.

For those of you who buy this book, not only will you be contributing towards the preservation of the local heritage, but you will also find that reading about the history of Torfaen communities can be a most informative and enjoyable experience.

Deborah Wildgust
Curator
Pontypool Museum

INTRODUCTION

With any writing project the general rule must be to convey unpublished raw material to the reader, but first, and a difficult hurdle to surmount, is the awareness of a new theme for the undertaking.

How fortunate I was when Deborah Wildgust, Curator of the Pontypool Museum, suggested that I write a book to commemorate the Golden Jubilee of Her Majesty Queen Elizabeth II and relate it to the Torfaen County Borough.

This gave the rare opportunity to link the past with the present, which, hopefully, will serve as a record of local people's admiration of the commitment and steadying presence of their remarkable Monarch.

Torfaen Museum Trust will receive the proceeds of this book.

W.G. Lloyd, 2002.

ACKNOWLEDGEMENTS

I wish to thank the following for their help in the research of this book:

Sue Allford
Wilf Bridges
Aubrey Collier
Florence Davies
Idris Davies
Derrick A. Dunning
Susan Dunning
Rosemary Easter
Betty Gallop
Cyril Irving
Lewis W. Jones
Kath Lapping
Gareth Lowe
Emma Richards
Ron Saunders
Paul Seabourne
Jay Skinner
Hazel Waters
Carol Ann Wells

Chapter One

The GOLDEN JUBILEE of QUEEN VICTORIA

R oyal Jubilees come and go with great excitement on the auspicious day. In no time at all the magnificent event is confined to the history books and often, with a lengthy period of time until the next great Royal event, some children will grow up without experiencing the huge anticipation of the special day. For those youngsters who would have the event firmly planted in their subconscious minds in readiness to tell their children and grandchildren, a souvenir may survive. In past times when young mothers cherished their glass display cabinets, often found in the best room of the house, the room used to entertain unexpected visitors, a commemorative mug or beaker would be observed amongst the delicate china objects. These souvenirs, often given to their young sons or daughters by the local school, would be held in the safe custody of the parent until the owner had reached maturity and married. Then, sometimes with tears flowing copiously, the family heirlooms would be handed over to the rightful owners in the hope that the next generation would appreciate not only the significance of the former Royal occasion, but also a time when their parents were experiencing the happiest period of their own young lives.

With only a few British monarchs reigning so long as fifty years, and very little recorded of their special year, it is interesting to observe that the Golden Jubilee of King George III appears to be the event which set the trend for future Royal celebrations. The event is splendidly reported in the following extracts from the Annual Register for 1809:

The happy event of a British monarch's entrance into the 50th year of his reign, an event which has occurred but twice before in the long and splendid history of this country, was celebrated by all ranks of people throughout every part of the United Kingdom, in a manner worthy of an amiable king, and a loyal and enlightened nation. The day was one of the finest imaginable for the season, and favoured the public expression of satisfaction in the highest degree. The celebration was announced in this great metropolis by the peeling of bells, the hoisting of flags, and the assembling of various bodies of regular troops, and the different corps of volunteers, throughout the town. The forenoon was dedicated in public worship in every parish church and chapel and all the shops were closed. The Lord Mayor and the whole civic body went in procession to St.

Paul's; and it was truly gratifying, amidst the multitudes in the streets, of both sexes and of every rank and description, to see the children of our innumerable charitable institutions walking to their respective places for divine worship...At one the Tower guns fired, and the guards assembled on parade in St. James's Park, and fired in honour of the event. After church hours, the streets were crowded with the population of the metropolis, in decent or lively attire; every house pouring forth its inhabitants, the number of well-dressed persons, and the display of the genuine beauty of a greater majority of the sex, who do not constantly shine at midnight dances and the public show, but whom this celebration brought into public view, exceeded any former example. Most of them wore ribbons of garter blue, and many had medals of the profile of the King.

The magnificent preparations of the evening were the general objects of notice, which the serenity of such a day as October does not often see gave them full opportunity of observing, while the volunteer corps, returning from their respective parades, enlivened the scene with a martial as well as patriotic and a festive feature. As the evening approached, the corporation of London and various other bodies were hastening to the Mansion House, and to their different halls, taverns and other places of meeting, to celebrate in a mirthful way the 50th year of the reign of a British king... Daylight was scarcely gone when the full blaze burst forth upon the evening in all the skill of art, and in all the radiant splendour and varied magnificence of the general illuminations of the British capital. Hands could hardly be procured to light up the innumerable lamps; and therefore the illuminating of most of the public edifices commenced as early as two in the afternoon. Many other customary demonstrations of popular satisfaction were abundantly exhibited...at Windsor the Royals proceeded to view the roasting of the ox. The butchers employed in managing the cooking dressed upon this occasion in blue frocks and silk stockings, cut the first prime pieces from the ox and put them upon silver plates before waiting upon the Royal party.

Thus the platform was set for future Jubilee celebrations.

Very early on the morning of June 20th, 1837, King William IV died at Windsor Castle. As he left no direct heirs the crown of the United Kingdom passed to his niece, the Princess Victoria, who was then eighteen years of age.

Before five o'clock on the morning of the King's death, two gentlemen, dusty and travelled-stained, arrived at Kensington Palace where Princess Victoria was living with her mother. They were William Howley, Archbishop of Canterbury, and Francis, Marquis of Conyngham, the Lord Chamberlain, who had travelled post-haste from

Windsor to inform the Princess of her accession. They knocked and rang for some time before they succeeded in awakening the sleeping household. At last a maidservant came down, and admitted them to a waiting room. The attendants of the Princess, being ignorant of the importance of the errand, were unwilling to waken her. The Archbishop and his companion were consequently kept waiting for more than an hour. It was not until they announced that they had come on business to *The Queen,* that her mother awakened Victoria.

She then came to them at once, in her dressing gown and slippers, a shawl thrown over her shoulders, and her hair hanging down. At the words, "Your Majesty," her eyes filled with tears, but she received the news of her accession with great dignity. "I ask your Grace's prayers on my behalf," she said gravely to the Archbishop.

Some hours later she presided at her first Council, and took the customary oaths. The dignified bearing of the girl-Queen astonished all the Ministers present. Thus began that great reign which was to be the longest and one of the most wonderful in the annals of our history.

The Princess Victoria, the only child of Edward Duke of Kent, the fourth son of King George III, was born at Kensington Palace on May 24th, 1819. Her father died the following year, and her widowed mother carefully brought up the Princess. The Duchess of Kent taught her daughter to be self reliant, truthful, brave, and considerate of the feelings of others. These characteristics she retained throughout her long life. She was also trained to practise economy, as though she had been born poor. As a little girl she would often be seen playing in Kensington Gardens, very simply dressed in a white cotton frock.

There was at first little expectation that the Princess would ever succeed to the throne, for she had two uncles whose heirs would have a prior claim. But George IV's only child, the Princess Charlotte, died at the age of twenty-one; and when he was succeeded by his brother William IV, who had no heir, the people of England began to look on the Princess as their future Queen. Until the time of her accession however, she and her mother lived quietly at Kensington Palace, and were seldom seen at Court.

The ceremony of Queen Victoria's coronation took place in Westminster Abbey, on June 28th, 1838. When the young Queen, wearing her crown, afterwards drove back to Buckingham Palace through the streets of London, she was hailed with such cheers has had not greeted any sovereign for many generations. The accession of the young Queen brought to an end the Hanoverian connexion, which had existed since 1714, for the Hanoverian crown could only pass to a male descendent. Ernest, Duke of Cumberland, the Queen's uncle, became King of Hanover.

On February 10th, 1840, Queen Victoria was married to her cousin, Prince Albert of Saxe-Cobourg, the second son of her mother's eldest brother. The union proved a very happy one. The Prince Consort, as he was styled, was handsome, accomplished, and worthy to be the husband of the noble young Queen.

There would be no Silver Jubilee celebration for Queen Victoria. A few years earlier, in 1861, her beloved Albert had died and her grief was inconsolable for many years to follow.

The year 1887, in the district now called Torfaen, began with little thought to the nearness of a great celebration about to witnessed in the summer months. The weather was bitterly cold, so cold that the bell ringers of Trevethin Church did not venture out for the townsfolk to hear the gladsome peal of bells speeding the departure of the old and welcoming the New Year. Those of a dedicated nature attended the New Year's Eve watch service in each chapel and church in the district and although a dense fog prevailed, it did not prevent some from enjoying their celebratory dinners and other pleasurable gatherings. Groups of music lovers made themselves heard while parading the streets and in the absence of the sounds of church bells, the shrill notes of 'hooters' from the district's collieries heralded in the special year.

It was a bleak beginning to the year. While many indulged in skating games on the thick ice covering the canal and local ponds, others were not so fortunate. A heavy fall of snow raised very little excitement among the young who had no suitable shoes to venture out. Distress caused by a long continued depression in trade generally was worsened by the stoppage of the local tin works. The folk in Trosnant, Pontymoile and Sowhill appeared to be the worse affected. Their failure to provide for a rainy day while wages were being drawn would soon be witnessed by cheerless homes and empty larders. A woman with three children would regularly tramp fifteen miles to get food for her offspring. Returning home she would be footsore and heart-broken from the numerous snubs hurled at her during the trek. Tradesmen, and even publicans, experienced a drop in receipts during these early months and had it not been for several philanthropic gentlemen who organised the Park Estate soup kitchen, the number of deaths in the Torfaen district would have been more numerous.

As the year progressed the dark clouds of despondency would to some extent roll by and the awakening to a great event became evident. The main reason for this was the appearance of advertisements proclaiming 'Monster Jubilee Festivities in Pontypool Park.' These advertisements were to appear not only in the Monmouthshire newspapers, but also in journals all around the country. The intention to raise little Pontypool from the oblivion of which it had sunk truly worked due to the exertions of one man, the town's fire chief, Captain Gus Bevan. Here was a man of tremendous energy and good management skills, his only failing being the lack of knowledge in financial matters. While the town of Newport commenced three highly successful subscription lists, which gave an indication of how much to spend on events and what would be left over to promote a good cause, the captain did a remarkable job of

4

MONSTER JUBILEE
FESTIVITIES !!
PONTYPOOL PARK.

Easter Monday, April 11th.

£1,200 to be Spent!!

Patrons: The Most Hon. The Marquess of Bute, &c.

The Greatest Musical
EISTEDDFOD !!
ever held.   FIRST PRIZE, £900.

ROASTING A ROYAL OX!!
Obtained from Her Majesty the Queen:
He will be roasted whole in full view of the visitors.

ILLUMINATED   FOUNTAINS!!

BLONDIN !!
The Hero of Niagara: Two Grand Performances.

BANDS! PLENTY OF SHELTER!!

VARIETY ENTERTAINMENT!!

FIRE PORTRAIT OF THE QUEEN!!

DINNER TO 3,000 POOR PEOPLE!!

FIREWORKS!!
The Full Crystal Palace Fête Display.

☞ This is the Greatest Entertainment ever Offered in the whole World we believe, and all at the Price below.

Admission to the whole of the above—
Only 1s.   Children—HALF PRICE.

⁎ For Trains from Ross, Monmouth, Lydbrook, Raglan, Usk, Abergavenny, &c., &c., see Railway Bills. Extra Accommodation for Horses and Traps provided in the Shepherds Field, near the House Entrance.

GUS BEVAN,
Captain Eire Brigade.

The County Observer, April 2, 1887.

5

organising, but to some extent left the gathering in of monies to Providence. Captain Bevan had on eight previous occasions organised successful fetes to raise funds for the voluntary fire brigade, and the previous year his team commendably raised a record sum of over £600. However, from a financial standpoint, the Jubilee Fete was a far different event and involved the payment of large amounts of money for entertainments, food and many other sundries, which any gigantic event would require.

Not only was money scarce at this time, but also the competition for the little amount available became intense. A letter sent by the Prince of Wales to the Lord Lieutenant of Monmouthshire caused copies to be forwarded to the Pontypool, Blaenafon, Abersychan and Panteg Local Boards. The content of the letter and other appeals put further pressure on the finances of each district:

> *Marlborough House*
> *Pall Mall*
> *S.W.*

Dear Sir,

    I have no doubt that your attention has been drawn to the correspondence which has recently passed between the Lord Mayor of London and myself on the subject of the formation of an Imperial Institution of the Colonies and India, in commemoration of Her Majesty's Jubilee by Her subjects, and to the opening of a Central Fund at the Mansion House in London for the receipt of contributions from various parts of the Empire towards this object.

    So I am convinced that the anxiety to commemorate in some special manner Her Majesty's Jubilee is felt warmly in the Provincial Cities and Towns of the United Kingdom as in any portion of the Queen's Dominions. I am desirous of wishing the cooperation of the Mayor's Provost, and Chairman of Sanitary Boards, in bringing the proposal prominently to the knowledge of their fellow townsmen, and in taking such practical steps, by the convening of meetings, the formation of local Committees, and the opening of local subscription lists, as many as may be desirable or necessary in aid of the Central Fund.

    It will give me much satisfaction to hear that I may count upon your personal assistance in the matter, and to learn from time to time how the fund is progressing.

> *I am Sir Your obedient servant,*
> *Albert Edward P.*

In keeping with their natural talents, the ladies of Torfaen were quick off the mark with raising money for a good cause. A recent national movement commenced which had for its objective the presentation to the Queen of a personal Jubilee offering from the women and girls of the United Kingdom as a mark of the loyal appreciation of her public and private character. The movement to be known as *'The Women's Jubilee Offering Movement'* was non-political, appealing to women and girls of all ages, classes and creeds to join in one common offering to their Queen in token of loyalty, affection, and reverence towards the only female sovereign in history who, for 50 years, had born the toils and troubles of public life, as a wife, mother and ruler. Any offering ranging from a penny to one pound was appreciated and the names of contributors would be presented to the Queen. When the huge project was completed, Her Majesty would be invited to decide upon the form the accumulated offering would take, although rumour had it that part of the donated money would provide an equestrian statue in the grounds of Windsor Castle.

Committees formed in every district in Torfaen and wealthy ladies organised the door-to-door collectors while provided them with an identification card. At first they met little response to their grand mission. Thought to be begging by the male members of most households and informed that the cause had nothing to do with them many doors would immediately close. Not to be put off, the determined agents would call again at a later time when they knew each husband was at his workplace.

Local interest increased especially when Jubilee souvenirs began to appear in the shops. The proprietor of the Swan Hotel, Pontypool, added to the increasing excitement when he offered a prize of £1 to the person who made the best estimate of the number of people attending the Jubilee Fete in Pontypool on Easter Monday. New coinage appeared with the Queen's portrait more in accordance with her Jubilee age than that of the young girl, which had been used for the previous fifty years. From late March, gold and silver medals to be competed for in the forthcoming Jubilee Eisteddfod, could be seen in the shop window of Fowlers, Commercial Street, Pontypool. These fascinated young children who were now fully aware that something exciting was about to happen which would allow them time off from school.

Months of hard work by Captain Bevan were at last reaching a culmination. He headed a committee of firemen who were each delegated a department involved in the festival and would report back on the progress of the final arrangements. Mrs Bevan gave tremendous support and hardly commented on the fact that her home had, for some months, been turned into something, which resembled a bill-posters establishment.

Mr. J.C. Hanbury, a descendant of the founder of the Pontypool iron industry, in his usual kind nature, gave permission for his parks to be used as a venue for the event and was appointed president of the Eisteddfod. Elaborate planning ensured that the Eisteddfod would be held in a separate area to the many other events. This involved platforms and an elaborate setting up in what was known as the Home Park, found immediately in front of the luxurious Hanbury residence. The completion of a temporary building for the traditional roasting of a Royal ox on a spit gave further indication to the general public of the events to follow. Purchased from Queen Victoria's Devon estate for the price of £39 19s 3d, the beast became an unwilling star in the proceedings. Under the supervision of a team of Pontypool butchers, who were headed by Messrs Richard Lloyd and T. Williams, the splendid animal was located in a stable behind the Wheatsheaf, in the market ground. In full view of a large number of curious sightseers, his fine proportions were not a little admired by many of the farmers and butchers. With so much interest in the animal being apparent, a railway journey to Newport gave the residents of that large town an opportunity to see the pride of Pontypool. Following a tour around the principle streets of Pontypool and district, and after years of basking in the Royal sunshine, a short trip to the slaughterhouse would result in an ignominious death at the hands of the ruthless local butchers.

Everything went like clockwork. Temporary extensions were erected to the town's railway stations to allow the expected huge numbers of travelling public easy entry into the town. Over sixty police officers, some mounted, would occupy a temporary barracks with cells in the park. The lower Deer Park was a sea of canvas, where could be located entertainments and provisions to help the non-musical masses through the long day. Finally, no more preparation could be undertaken. Everything now depended on the weather.

Once more the croakers - the prophets of evil - were doomed to disappointment as Easter Monday dawned to the accompaniment of typical spring weather. Before nine o'clock the first special train containing visitors arrived, and the service continued with almost ceaseless activity until mid-day. By ten o'clock the commercial part of the town was full to capacity. Each tradesman had made a magnificent effort to decorate their premises with flags and bunting proudly proclaiming the year of the Jubilee. It was reported, "the streets were instinct with life and bright with animation, and still the stream of sightseers and songsters, from distant Burslem, Wrexam and Llanelly, continued to pour into the town."

Around £300 had been put by for prizes and medals ready for the Eisteddfod. Visiting choirs and musical performers would find their way to an allocated chapel for a last minute rehearsal before entering the park and performing in front of an audience containing the elite of the district. The test piece selected was *"Wretched Lovers"* from *"Acis and Galatea."* With the participants being old eisteddfod foes, the first prize of £200 went to Dowlais, and the second to Llanelly, with Burslem receiving an enthusiastic burst of applause.

The gigantic undertaking in the park caused all previous events in Pontypool to pale into insignificance. Thousands watched the events in the Deer Park. People sat on the adjacent hill, whilst higher still, "far from the maddening crowd," were hundreds of couples who looked utterly unlike the *"Wretched Lovers"* visualised so intently in the nearby canvas dome. Chevalier Blondin again worked his magic on the high wire. Famous for his repeated tightrope crossings of the Niagara Falls, he made two appearances. A trick that caused great applause occurred when he covered the full length of high wire somehow framed by colourful fireworks.

An ascent in a balloon by local dignitaries thoroughly amused the large crowd, while a representation of the *"Bombardment of Alexandria,"* followed by a diorama, with limelight effect, and musical clowns, all added to the diversity of the programme. The children were further amused by the presence of Studt's Fair, which used its roundabouts and swing boats to great advantage.

The Pontypool butchers responded magnificently on this special day. Acting chiefly as cooks, they worked in relays and under a regular scrutiny of spectators whose expressions testified in unmistakable terms to their desire for a closer acquaintance with the flesh of the splendid animal. Many commented in passing that they had discharged their duty in a most laudable manner, the huge "joint" having been done "to a turn." A part of the Royal ox would survive. Mr. J.C. Hanbury later presented a hoof, mounted in gold, to Her Majesty in the form of an inkstand.

The end to a memorable day came with a superb display of Japanese fireworks, and a fire-portrait of the Queen. Soon, after the bands played the National Anthem, the satisfied visitors streamed from the park and made their way home. It had been a rare day in the annals of the history of Pontypool. Over 80,000 visitors had arrived in Pontypool and thanks mostly to the tireless work of Captain Bevan, not one accident had occurred and no serious bad behaviour was reported. He had been the first to have the idea of promoting a Jubilee Fete and all around the country, towns and villages followed his lead.

A few days later the planned treat for the poor was given in Pontypool Park. Between 2000-3000 people were served with the flesh of the Royal ox or a variety of other mouth-watering foodstuffs. On that day all the hard work seemed worthwhile to an exhausted Captain Bevan. As he relaxed in his fireside chair as night descended, he

Jubilee Ox, Pontypool Market, 1887.

1887 Jubilee Fete, Lower Deer Park, Pontypool.

Leading the ox through the streets of Pontypool. Inset shows Captain Gus Bevan, chief officer of Pontypool Steam Fire Brigade and organiser of the fete.

Roasting the ox.

The Eisteddfod.

*Steam Fire engines pumping water to make ornamental fountains.
Inset shows Mr. J.C. Hanbury, squire of Pontypool.*

looked once more at the telegram he received that morning from Sir Henry Ponsonby, Her Majesty's secretary. It read: *"The Queen much gratified, and returns her thanks for kind congratulations."*

The Jubilee Fete and treat for the poor had been a huge success. Without any subscription list, financial help from the Local Board, or anyone voluntary digging deep into their pockets, the Torfaen district still had a wonderful time without any cost. With money obtained from entrance fees, Captain Bevan immediately settled all expenses. Unfortunately the money to commence a free library or a new fire brigade station had not been raised. The cost of things had run up and with a number of bad debts the amount raised would still be a useful £192 17s 5d, but not enough for any major memorial project. From this amount £50 would be given to the voluntary fire brigade for a new hose, and at the time, as the idea of a free library did not excite the slightest interest in the neighbourhood, the remainder was placed in a bank account for a future library site.

Pontypool and district remained in a festive mood. With the official Golden Jubilee Day planned for June 21st, the streets of the old town remained a sea of flags, bunting and numerous portraits of Queen Victoria. A Jubilee concert at the Pontypool Town Hall by the scholars of Pontymoile National School would prove to be a huge success. Attended by the privileged of Torfaen, the scholars would perform well in front of a profuse display of symbolic devices and appropriate mottoes, one of the latter bearing the inscription, "Victoria R.I., 1837-1887." In keeping with its well-earned national fame, on May 24th, a specially erected new flag fluttered cheerfully from the Pontypool Town Hall to celebrate the Queen's birthday.

To the delight of the schoolchildren, the schools in Torfaen broke up for a week to celebrate the Golden Jubilee. In all the schools the children had mustered strongly for a short period in anticipation of the treats promised for the following week. In the districts, the collectors had worked hard, subscription lists were full, and the wealthy coal and iron proprietors had dug deep into their pockets. Everything was ready for a great occasion.

On June 20th, 1887, Queen Victoria had reigned for fifty years. Among British sovereigns only Henry III, Edward III, and George III, had reigned for so long a period. On June 21st, her Jubilee was celebrated with great rejoicing in all parts of her dominions. In India 25,000 prisoners were released in honour of the great day. The children in every school in the British Empire had a holiday.

The chief event of the Jubilee was the Thanksgiving Service in Westminster Abbey. The Queen, accompanied by her children and grandchildren, attended by a brilliant escort of foreign Princes, drove to the Abbey through the gaily-decorated streets. In the procession were the troops from all parts of the Empire, and Indian Princes in colourful costumes.

The procession was witnessed by the largest number of persons that had assembled in the streets of London. Since the commencement of the Queen's reign, railways and steamboats had made rapid conveyance possible, and crowds of visitors poured into London for the great occasion from all parts of the country.

Within the Abbey there was gathered a congregation of 10,000 people, drawn from almost every part of the world. The Queen sat in the chair of Edward I, in which fifty years before, when a young, untried girl she had been crowned Queen. A short and simple Thanksgiving Service was held.

For Torfaen, it was a joyous day.

In the afternoon, the scholars of Henllys Board School, Cwmbran, were regaled with cake and tea, by the generosity of Mr. and Mrs. E. Southwood Jones, of Henllys House. They were met on the lawn by Mr. and Mrs. Jones and after a few words the children adjourned to an adjoining field where they indulged in various games. Two swings had been erected for the occasion, one for the girls and one for the boys. For the amusement of everyone, a tug of war competition between the men from the colliery and brickworks resulted in a win for the colliers. Over a hundred prizes were subsequently awarded for various contests, which included three-legged and wheelbarrow races. The eventful afternoon ended with three cheers for Mr. and Mrs. Jones.

The young inmates at the Griffithstown Workhouse were to receive a double treat on the special day. It was readily agreed by the Board of Guardians that a dinner of roast beef and plum pudding, the same as at Christmas, would be given, while the men received an additional pint of beer and two ounces of tobacco. The ladies received the equivalent in tea and sugar instead of the usual ounce of snuff. In the afternoon the children of Sebastopol and Griffithstown walked past shops and businesses adorned with a profuse display of flags and bunting. An influential committee, headed by Mr. Isaac Butler, ironmaster, had organised a treat for the children and a large number of poor and aged, which was to be pleasantly remembered for many years. A triumphal arch erected in honour of the occasion on the canal bridge at Griffithstown gave a "Welcome to all children," particularly those from the Workhouse, as they all walked to a field below the Panteg Works. Here they were regaled with tea, cake, and bread and butter, the cost of which was defrayed by public subscription. Nearby in the schoolroom of the Pontymoile National School, two hundred poor and aged sat down to a sumptuous dinner. As part of the occasion, Mr. Butler ordered two thousand medals, which were to be distributed to scholars through the Sunday Schools in the district.

The weather was magnificent for Jubilee Day in Pontypool. It was without a doubt a golden day, but a repetition of Easter Monday's success would be impossible. In the main it was felt that the celebration should be left in the hands of private individuals. The memorable day was to some extent ushered in with mixed feelings. Shortly after midnight, when most of the townsmen were dreaming of the past or future, the Hanbury Band commenced playing the ever-popular National Anthem outside a beer house in George Street. The instrumental arrangement was supplemented by a vocalisation, the singers being augmented by a large number of persons who had at that late-or-early hour been attracted to the spot by the unusual proceedings. Lusty cheers were afterwards given for Her Majesty. During the day even more streamers seemed to span the streets, and flags and Union Jacks were in profusion. In order to attend a Thanksgiving Service at Trevethin Church, the children of the Sunday Schools met at the Town School, and headed by a band, marched in procession through the streets with flags waving. After the service each child was presented with a souvenir prayer book to commemorate the historic day. Many of the inhabitants wended their way to the park where advantage would be taken of the splendid weather for picnics and games. Elsewhere parties of a public or private character were plentifully patronised.

At Pontnewynydd, Abersychan and Garndiffaith large donations enabled a fine treat for each district supported by many helping hands. The preparation of food in Garndiffaith and Talywain could not be surpassed anywhere in the Torfaen valley. Famous for their pastry cooking, the ladies had been covered in flour for about a week previously. On conclusion of the tea, the children were sent to Dr. Mulligan's field, near Talywain railway station. Here, eighteen swings had been especially erected for the children and a large number of games were entered into.

A new fire engine was planned to be the centrepiece of the lavish Blaenafon Jubilee celebrations and the Local Board experienced a great deal of anxiety while waiting for it to be delivered. Repeated correspondence to the makers, Merryweather and Son, urged immediate delivery. Thankfully, the handsome, bright red, horse drawn vehicle arrived a few days before the important celebration. Weighing 1 ton and 17 cwts, the coveted engine cost £103 3s 0d and can still be seen at the Pontypool Museum, where it was restored at great expense. The special day in the busy little town would eclipse anything known in the memory of the oldest inhabitant. In a short time a fund of £220 had been raised. In readiness for the unique day the residents became daring with their presentation of decorations, in fact every vantage point was used for the purpose of adornment. Scarlet was the principle colour employed in the decorations, whilst flags and streamers, ensigns and Union Jacks floated everywhere. A large new flag fluttered from the top of St. Peter's Church, the bells of which rang out merrily during most of the day. The planned programme began with a procession, formed in the Blaenafon Park and which left in the following order: -

Representatives of the Gloucestershire Yeomanry
Ministers of various Denominations
Choir
British School Children
Choir
Wesleyan School Children
Members of the Iron and Workers Fund
Band
Volunteers
Members of the Tradesmen's Fund
Choir
Forge Side Board School Children
Roman Catholic School Children
Members and Officers of the Local Board
Fire Brigade
Tradesmen of the Town
Choir
Blaenafon and Pwlldu National School Children

The procession, which numbered over 4,000, took more than half-an-hour to pass a given point. When returning to the park everyone gathered in front of a platform in order to witness the christening ceremony of the new fire engine. Confidently raising a bottle of wine attached by a ribbon to the engine, Mrs. R.W. Kennard said, "I have great pleasure in christening this engine the 'John Worton.'" Following musical renditions and singing by the choirs, everyone moved to nearby Park House Field where Mrs. Worton expertly planted a commemorative lime tree. By this time the children were hungry and eagerly went to their school for the expected hearty meal. The elderly folk were quite happy to attend the nearest hostelry for their free meal. Returning to the park, the rest of the day was thoroughly enjoyed by taking up games and competitions.

Everyone in Torfaen had truly enjoyed the rare and wonderful day. As darkness descended, people not tired by the genuine expressions of devotion to Her Majesty

Jubilee Building, Pontypool, with date stone.
Private dwelling erected in 1887.

Queen Victoria, found a vantage point to observe the Jubilee bonfires. Monmouthshire was well represented in the chain of beacons nation wide and ablaze by 10 p.m.

It had been a wonderful time in Torfaen with only the Pontypool Town Hall clock appearing to lack any involvement in the exciting events. Perhaps fired by the stimulating ringing of church bells in the district during the previous day, it became determined to indulge in a late Jubilee celebration of its own. After striking the hour of three in the afternoon, the clock continued to exercise itself in a similar manner for upwards of over half-an-hour, during which time it had, to the amusement of all who heard the eccentricity, struck something like 660 o'clock. Mr. Loeffler, watchmaker and custodian, could not account for the late contribution to the historic celebrations.

Immediately after Golden Jubilee Day, a supplement in the *London Gazette* was published and contained a letter From the Queen. The same letter appeared in the Monmouthshire newspapers in the days that followed:

> *"Windsor Castle, June 24th, 1887.*
> *"I am anxious to express to my people my warm thanks for the kind, and more than kind, reception I met with on going to and returning from Westminster Abbey, with my children and grandchildren.*
> *"The enthusiastic reception I met with then, as well as on all these eventful days, in London as well as Windsor, on the occasion of my jubilee, has touched me most deeply. It has shown that the labour and anxiety of fifty long years, twenty of which I spent in unclouded happiness shared and cheered by my beloved husband, while an equal number were full of sorrow and trials borne without a sheltering arm and wise help, have been appreciated by my people.*
> *"This feeling, and the sense of duty towards my dear country and subjects who are so inseparably bound up with my life, will encourage me in my task – often a very difficult and arduous one – during the remainder of my life.*
> *"The wonderful order preserved on this occasion, and the good behaviour of the enormous multitudes assembled merit my highest admiration.*
> *"That God may protect and abundantly bless my country is my fervent prayer.*
> *VICTORIA R and I."*

Queen Victoria devoted the greatest part of the money raised by *The Woman's Jubilee Offering Fund* to a scheme for providing trained nurses for the poor and on July 14th she laid the foundation stone of the Imperial Institute.

Chapter Two

The Diamond Jubilee of Queen Victoria

T he Diamond Jubilee held in 1897, on completion of the sixtieth year of Queen Victoria's reign, would be more wonderful than anything previously experienced in the United Kingdom. Still remembered as achieving national fame for the Golden Jubilee celebrations, Pontypool and district would again join in wholeheartedly. People were now observing a record-breaking reign, which deserved the attention its uniqueness brought with it. No doubt children witnessing the event would, when grey headed, be telling their grandchildren of the special time and for most, the event would not be repeated during their lives.

Mr. J.C. Hanbury got things off to an early start when, without prompting, he kindly offered the delightful grounds of Pontypool Park House for the Jubilee celebrations. This offer was indeed a bonus to the proceedings from the very beginning as the general public rarely had the privilege of visiting the private grounds to see the fairest of nature's creations, and enjoy the delicious sensations, which the communion with the beautiful always gives. Exploratory meetings throughout Torfaen discussed in-depth the various programmes to make it a memorable year in the valley. Sadly, Captain Gus Bevan would play no part in the proceedings. Poor health had hastened his retirement to Jersey, where he passed away a few years later. However, there would be plenty of willing hands available. The ladies immediately took up the task of collecting money for providing a treat for the children and aged poor. A sensible arrangement had been reached to raise the amount to first cover the costs of the treats, and to make a later appeal for donations for a new Literary Library to serve as a permanent reminder in Torfaen of a great moment in history.

The organisation of the Whit-Monday Jubilee Fete commenced under a capable committee. Many at the time would remember Blondin, the star of the 1887 celebration. In February 1897, the hero of Niagara, as he was known, died at his home in Ealing, London, age 75 years. However, a new star had emerged and would adequately head the Pontypool bill. Menotti had become the premier high-wire act and Torfaen was lucky to have his services. This artiste had not appeared in the valley before, but his exhibition in other parts of the country had already won him national fame. A Liverpool newspaper, in speaking of his appearance at the New Star Musical Hall, said: -

"Menotti, as the central attraction, has this week been electrifying crowded houses at the Music Hall in the Square by his intrepid aerial exploits. The public is not unused to the spectacle of artistes of a certain class having their names blazoned amid a flourish of high-sounding epithets – "the great," the "world's champion," the "idol of the people," the "gem of comedy," and so on, through the gamut of bumptious phraseology, and also it may be remarked the public is much more amused by this parade of names than entertained by the originals themselves. But no one who has seen Menotti, not even the most captious, would quarrel for a moment with his designation as the Stockholm Wonder."

Money was quickly raised to cover all expenses. The only competition for subscriptions was the worthy collection for a county hospital at Newport. The *South Wales Argus* newspaper commenced a well-patronised "Shilling Fund" in the hope that the new hospital would prevent people from all over Monmouthshire having to travel to Bristol and other distant medical centres.

Much to the relief of the children in the district the Whit-Monday Jubilee Fete arrived to the accompaniment of fine weather in the beautiful grounds. Excursion trains brought hundreds of spectators from various parts of the country. After visiting the commercial area of the town bedecked with decorations of every description they made for the fete. The park gates were thrown open at eleven o'clock and by one o'clock about 5,000 people were strolling around enjoying the scenery. This number would be further augmented until a large concourse of people was in position for the attractions to begin.

The attractions were varied, but one was by far more intense than all the others. It would be the Stockholm Wonder who drew the gasps from the crowd and caused many a lady to shield their eyes in anticipation of witnessing a terrible calamity. In place of the heavy rope he used a length of wire only an eighth of an inch in thickness. His feats consisted of the following: Walking across the wire both forwards and backwards with a balancing pole; walking blindfolded while enveloped in a sack, and swaying violently from side to side; walking the wire without the pole; skating across on blade skates; carrying a man on his back; and riding across on a bicycle backwards and forwards with a balancing pole. Each demonstration of tremendous nerve and skill would bring forth from the huge crowd a vociferous cheer and no one was in any doubt that they were watching a master of the high wire.

Donkey races, brass band competitions, sports, horse jumping competitions, and a host of side shows supplemented the main attraction and caused the afternoon to pass far too quickly. The evening brought a mellow period with dancing to the band of the

3rd Volunteer Battalion, South Wales Borderers, under the leadership of Mr. S.T. Roderick. At not too late an hour, and for the convenience of the children present, a firework display, which included a fire portrait of Her Majesty, concluded a wonderful Jubilee Fete in Pontypool Park.

More was to be enjoyed with a special Jubilee Day set aside for June 22nd. In the meantime, enterprising Torfaen folk travelled the short distance to Newport to admire the new Royal Jubilee Train specially built by the Great Western Railway Company for the Queen during her momentous year. Visiting Newport on a trial trip, a large number of spectators assembled on High Street Station to await its arrival. The train was everything the enthusiasts hoped it would be. It consisted of the Royal carriage, two saloons, one corridor first carriage, and two vans, one at each end for cooking light refreshments. All were painted on the outside in the distinctive Royal colours. The train spent some time in a nearby siding to allow engineers to inspect the carriages and a further perusal by the youngsters among the interested sightseers.

The Diamond Jubilee celebrations in London exceeded everyone's hopes. Celebrations were devised to show the wonderful expansion of the Empire during the Queen's reign. Colonial delegates met at a conference to discuss such questions as imperial defence and trade within the Empire. It was arranged that Prime Ministers from all the colonies, delegates from India and the dependencies, and representatives of all the armed forces of the British Empire, should take a prominent part in the procession to and from St. Paul's Cathedral, on June 22nd, when a short Thanksgiving Service was to be held on the steps at the west end of the Cathedral.

The procession to the Cathedral was the most magnificent ever witnessed in London. Preceded by a hundred men of the Royal Navy rode detachments of British Life Guards, Royal Horse Artillery, Dragoons, Hussars, Lancers, and the Imperial Service Troops serving in India. Then came the carriages with Guards and outriders, containing the children, grandchildren and great-grandchildren of the Queen, and foreign Princes from nearly every country in the world.

With the Prime Ministers from the self-governing colonies were troops from Newfoundland, New South Wales, Victoria, Queensland, South Australia, Western Australia, Tasmania, New Zealand and the Cape of Good Hope. They were followed by detachments of cavalry and infantry from Bengal, Bombay, and the Punjab, the flower of the great Indian army, many in dazzling uniforms. Nor was the smaller colonies unrepresented, for there were Chinese from Hong Kong, and dark-faced native police from the Straits Settlements, Sierra Leone, the Gold Coast, Trinidad, and the West Indies.

Queen Victoria attends Thanksgiving Service on the steps of St. Paul's Cathedral, 1897.

After these, rode the Princes of our own royal family, followed by foreign Sovereigns and Princes. Almost last of all there came a carriage in which was seated our aged Queen, acknowledging the greetings of millions of her subjects and baring bravely the burden of her seventy-eight years.

In the evening every British city was illuminated, and bonfires blazed from many a hill and headland not only in Britain, but also in India and her colonies, and even in foreign countries where British communities existed.

The Diamond Jubilee celebrations in Torfaen commenced with an enthusiastic send off to twenty part-time soldiers of the 3rd Volunteer Battalion, South Wales Borderers. Complete with haversacks, water bottles, pouch and great coats, the men were a credit to the battalion as they stood on the Pontypool railway station in readiness to commence their journey to the capital city. Here, the next day, they would march to Westminster Bridge to form a guard for the passing dignitaries.

The great day arrived in Torfaen without any immediate threat of rain. Perhaps to some extent the experience of the former great Jubilee ten years earlier had conditioned the local inhabitants to the anticipation of a wonderful day. Whereas, for the Golden Jubilee little was known of what to expect, on this occasion it was not left to one man to lead the way, but for hundreds to enthusiastically join in with the preparations.

The whole of Torfaen wore a holiday appearance. In every locality there was hardly a house from which flags and bunting was not displayed, whilst the early music from various bands gave warning of what was to come.

In Blaenafon a splendid day was spent. The Urban District Council decided not to take any action in the matter as a public body and the inhabitants rallied around to give everyone a day to remember. Many would remember the special services held at the parish church.

At Abersychan and district the collection books were full and the business and professional people in the area had donated most graciously. In the schools the children had their treats before breaking up for the Jubilee holiday. Another party on the special day, with the presentation of a souvenir enamelled steel mug and followed by lively games, caused many a youngster to sleep soundly that night.

The festivities in Pontypool began early with the part-time soldiers of the 3rd and 4th Volunteer Battalions, South Wales Borderers meeting up with the Panteg Artillery. After marching to the park, four of the guns belonging to the Artillery were fired and could be heard for a great distance. Visitors to the town found the principle streets extravagantly decorated as the result of so much enthusiasm. In the afternoon a substantial ham tea was given to the elderly poor in the district followed by tea and distribution of Jubilee mugs to over 2,000 children in the Market Hall. The united Sunday Schools of Pontypool and Pontnewynydd then marched to the park, where sports of various kinds were eagerly indulged in.

In the Panteg district the celebrations were carried out in capital style. Tea was provided at the schools in Sebastopol, Griffithstown, Pontymoile and New Inn, to all children less than fourteen years of age. This was followed by a presentation to those children on the school's register of a cup made of sheet steel, enamelled, and with a portrait of Her Majesty on the side. Also, the elderly poor of the district received a sum of money to use in their own way to join in the celebration. The children of all the schools then made their way to Pontypool Park in order to continue the festivities.

In the Griffithstown Workhouse it had been decided by the Pontypool Board of Guardians to give the inmates a special day by releasing them, as much as possible, from labour and providing a good dinner and tea with an extra allowance of tobacco

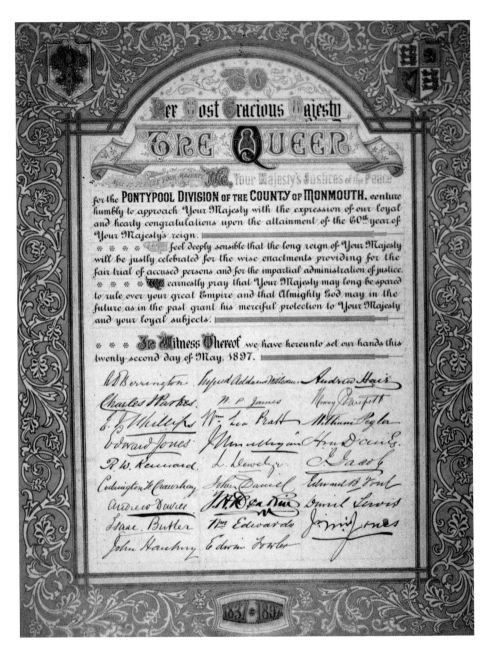

Pontypool's Royal address to Queen Victoria in 1897.

and snuff. A further benefit would be forthcoming when the outdoor relief increased by 1/- to every adult and 6d to every child on the previous day.

For some months a goodly number of visitors patronised the well-known Cwmbran Gardens hostelry, found alongside the Pontnewydd section of the Monmouthshire Canal. Already famous from as far off as Cardiff, where brakes and trains had brought customers for some years, the gaily-decorated establishment would do well during the Jubilee season.

In Pontnewydd, the children nearly had a bitter disappointment as a substantial donation to the new infirmary at Newport caused no public effort to be made for the festival. Fortunately, at a late date, a tea was arranged in the church and schools. After tea, games were organised in an adjoining field kindly loaned by Alderman H. Parfitt. Three cheers were given for Mr. Parfitt before the singing of the National Anthem ended the proceedings.

The works at Cwmbran became only partially operational during Jubilee week as Monday and Tuesday were observed as a general holiday in the neighbourhood. For some time a dark cloud had hung over the Jubilee proceedings in this old and respected district, but due to the kind offer of Mr. Clifford Cory, of Llantarnam Abbey, the gloom would be dispelled and the children experienced an exceptional Jubilee celebration. The event of the day was the visit to Llantarnam Park, the home of Mr. Cory. At one o'clock the children assembled at St. Dials, and headed by the Salvation Army band, marched with banners to the beautiful park. The younger children had the added treat of being carried to and fro in spacious and brightly coloured farm wagons. A large marquee had been erected in case the weather proved unfavourable, but the children were bountifully supplied with their refreshments on the fresh green sward, which helped not a little to their happiness and comfort. Nuts were scrambled for, and commemorative medals generously provided by Mr. Cory, were presented to each youngster. The lively proceedings concluded with the children singing "God Save the Queen."

The Volunteer soldiers of Torfaen had a hard, but interesting day on guard duty in London while witnessing the main Diamond Jubilee celebrations. Although disappointed in not being allowed to stay in London for the later illuminations, they had a splendid view of the numerous celebratory bonfires during the train journey home.

As darkness encompassed the valley the celebrations for many were by no means over. The beer houses over spilled with good-natured revellers determined to keep the celebration alive. In Pontypool the illuminations all added to the huge party. Immediately above the ironmonger's premises of Davies and Sandbrook was a picturesque and striking example of local talent. A large and flaming "V.R.," lit by over a hundred small electric bulbs became a main attraction. In Clarence Street, at the offices of the Gas and Water Company, a similar design, ornamented with a beautiful wreath and lit with gas caused children to gasp with wonder. Brilliant and powerful lights continued to light up most of the town until well into the next morning

As night fell bonfires were to be seen everywhere. An account in a Monmouthshire newspaper splendidly records for all time the never-to-be forgotten late night scene all those many years ago:

Proceeding from the Park at about 9 p.m., when everything had concluded and nothing was present to induce a further stay, the majority of those present wended their way to the Folly, on the Little Mountain, an eminence which commands a view unsurpassed for magnificence in the county. The commencement of festivities for here was announced for 11 o'clock, and those who reached their destination before this hour found much to divert their attention during the short time they had to wait. Ultimately the signal rocket was sent up and at this moment the band struck up the National Anthem. Then Mr. Nichols, to whose enterprise all was due, put the torch to the bonfire which was composed of furze, brushwood, barrels and tar, and which was surmounted with the flag of the nation. The inflammable material was but a second in igniting, and ere a couple of minutes had passed the flame reached a considerable height. From this time the attention of the spectators was occupied alternatively with watching the progress of the blaze round which they were gathered and with searching the surrounding hills for indications of festivities of a like character; and they had not far to look, for on every eminence was visible a bonfire, whilst even across the Bristol Channel could be seen the illuminations there displayed. Lines of vessels with brilliant lights could be seen in the channel; in fact the whole of the surrounding country presented an unexampled scene. Rockets, balloons, and coloured fires were then displayed, the band playing national airs the while. The light of the fire fell upon a dense mass of humanity, thousands upon thousands having gathered to witness what was to bring to a close that day of days. Milk sellers and stallholders plied a busy trade, and as the night wore on and people required refreshments, instances of the business capacity of the traders were shown, a penny a time only sufficing to purchase a glass of water. Subsequently, whilst the revelries and rejoicings were at their height, and the flames of the fire had somewhat diminished, the band played for dancing, large numbers engaging in this delightful occupation. The tower was also brilliantly illuminated with coloured lights, and this served to give even a brighter and more inspiring aspect to the surroundings. By 11 o'clock, however, the fireworks concluded, and an hour later the fire had lost the greater part of its power. Gathered around the diminished glow were still to be seen hundreds of people, but the more discreet and less enthusiastic had by this time departed, and those who still found entertainment were left on the scene, some singing the Queen's praises. Others engaged in pouring tales of love and devotion into each other's ears. And thus was brought to a close a day that must rank in the history of our town as one of the most glorious ever known, and as one never destined to be excelled.

LITERARY INSTITUTE
AND
READING ROOM,
PONTYPOOL.

President—J. C. HANBURY, ESQ., J.P., D.L.
Vice-Presidents—

REV.C. E.T. GRIFFITH, M.A.	I. BUTLER, ESQ., J.P.
REV. H. B. ROBINSON, FRGS.	H. BYTHWAY, ESQ.
REV. JOSHUA EVANS, M.A.	LEWIS E. WEBB, ESQ.
J. R. ESSEX, ESQ.	W. SANDBROOK, ESQ.

DIAMOND JUBILEE
PERMANENT MEMORIAL.

WE desire to solicit your hearty and practical sympathy with a movement which we are confident will commend itself to your judgment as a creditable and useful Permanent Memorial of the Diamond Jubilee. It will be remembered that on the 12th of May last a duly convened and largely-attended Town's Meeting was held in the Town Hall, and presided over by Mr. E. B. Ford, J.P., Chairman of the District Council, when it was proposed by Mr Donald Reid, President of the Chamber of Trade, and seconded by Mr. A. A. Williams, J.P. (Maesderwen). and carried unanimously :—

"That in the opinion of this meeting the "most desirable permanent means of locally "commemorating the Diamond Jubilee be the "provision of Public Reading Room, Library, "and Recreation Room over the Arcade Shops, "now in the course of erection by the District "Council, and that Subscriptions towards that "object should be solicited subsequent to "June 22nd."

Towards the cost of these rooms, which are now approaching completion, the Chamber of Trade generously voted £200, and an arrangement has been made with the District Council with respect to tenancy. The cost of suitably fitting-up and furnishing the rooms, however, will be considerably over £100, whilst it is most advisable also to make additions to the library. The Joint Committee, representing the Institute, the District Council, and the Chamber of Trade therefore venture to express the hope that you will generously respond to an appeal which has for its end the moral and intellectual advancement of the young people of the town and neighbourhood.

Signed for the Committee.
J. R. ESSEX,
Chairman of the Meeting ;
DONALD REID,
President of the Chamber of Trade ;
EDWD. B. FORD,
Chairman of the District Council ;
H. BERESFORD ROBINSON,
Secretary.

Subscriptions will be gladly received at the London and Provincial Bank and at Lloyds Bank.

1897 Literary Institute and Reading Room, Pontypool, with Datestone.

1897 Datestone.

Chapter Three

The SILVER JUBILEE of KING GEORGE V

K ing George V was born at Marlborough House on June 3rd, 1865. His brother Albert Victor, Duke of Clarence and Avondale, was his elder by a year and five months. Their father had determined that they should have a naval training, and sent them for two years to the *Britannia* at Dartmouth.

After leaving the *Britannia*, the Princes went for a three years' cruise on the *Bacchante*. On their return Prince George had acquired a zest for living. "Georgie is also much grown," recorded Queen Victoria in her diary, "He has still the same bright merry face as ever."

In 1892 he received his captaincy, but in the same year all his prospects were changed by the death of his brother. He had by this time an experience of fifteen years at sea, but as he was now in the direct line of succession, he could no longer continue his naval career.

Shortly after his brother's death Prince George was created Duke of York. On July 6th, 1893, he married the Princess Mary of Teck, who had been betrothed to his brother.

Queen Victoria, a few weeks before her death in 1901, signed a royal commission appointing the Duke of York to open the first Parliament of the Australian Commonwealth. King Edward VII on his accession desired that his son should carry out this arrangement. The Duke and Duchess sailed for Australia in the *Ophir* in March 1901. Following a magnificent welcome the ceremony of opening the Commonwealth Parliament took place in the Exhibition Hall at Melbourne on May 9th, in the presence of 12,000 spectators.

On leaving Australia the *Ophir* sailed across the Indian Ocean to Durban in Natal. At Pietermaritzburg a great gathering of Zulu and Kaffir chiefs assembled, the first of its kind ever received by a member of our royal family. They presented the Duke with an address, in which they referred to the death of the Great White Queen as the "setting of the sun which had left deep darkness over the land." The Duke, in his reply, said he was touched by their expression of grief, but he assured them that the sun had not set forever; it had now risen again in the reign of his father, who would watch over the chiefs and their people with unceasing care.

On November 2nd 1901, they returned to Great Britain, having accomplished one of the most important royal tours in the history of the Empire. They had been absent seven months, and had travelled 47,000 miles without once setting foot on any soil that was not part of the British Empire.

In the following year King Edward, on his birthday (November 9th), created his son Prince of Wales. As India had not been visited in the Australian tour, the Prince and Princess of Wales made a special journey to visit Australia and Burma in 1906. The future king had indeed received a worthy preparation by the time of his accession.

Proclamation of King George V at Blaenafon, 1910

The Prince, as King George V, succeeded to the British throne on the death of his father, in 1910. The Coronation of King George and Queen Mary took place in Westminster Abbey on June 22nd, 1911 in the presence of a large assembly of distinguished guests from all parts of the world.

King George V had five sons and one daughter. Prince John sadly died at the age of thirteen. The King became a home lover, and most warmly attached to his wife and children. Neither he nor the Queen cared much about the gaieties of society. Inclined to be a good speaker, his travels had given him a wide knowledge of men and cities. Always, he would take the keenest possible interest in all matters that affected the welfare of his subjects, and his vast Empire. His reign proved a critical period in the history of his people. During the years of the Great War, His Majesty gave a splendid lead to the nation, and set a high example of courage and perseverance.

In 1924, Prince Edward, the Prince of Wales, visited Torfaen to attend the hugely supported National Eisteddfod of Wales, held in Pontypool Park. In time for the popular events the handsomely constructed new town bridge leading to Trevethin would be officially opened by Major-General Lord Treowen, C.B., C.M.G., Lord Lieutenant of the County. In fine weather the ceremony went well and during his address Lord Treowen reminded everyone of the bardic title, 'Iorwerth Dywysog,' which the young Prince would receive at the festival. He went on to suggest that they named the new bridge the "Pont Iorwerth Dywysog" in honour of the royal visit. The suggestion met with great applause and all present approved of the new name.

Despite difficult economic times the people of Torfaen were truly interested in celebrating the Silver Jubilee of their popular King. The various councils although short of money, thought the people, particularly the children, should have something special to take their minds off the gloom the hard times had brought.

Numerous ideas and newspaper reports at the beginning of 1935 caused awareness to blossom. The appearance of Jubilee medals, sold at 2s 6d in fine silver for a small one and one guinea for a large, excited those who could afford to buy. The obverse side showed the King and Queen and the other side showed Windsor Castle surrounded by the Latin inscription, "Stet Fortuna Domus." The ladies fashion shops in the valley began to follow the lead of those in London by selling garments in red, white and blue. These cheerful, patriotic colours soon became popular and the spring costumes in Jubilee blue became a must among the Torfaen ladies. For the recently formed radio company of Rediffusion, the event would be a huge bonus. Sales had soured through the previous Christmas speech of the King and now advertisements informed prospective customers that they could not only listen to the commentary on May 6th, but also hear the mighty cheers as the King went by, and the horses passing. It was a great temptation to join the scheme when assured that the listeners only had to close their eyes and they would believe they were at the London celebrations. Children began to take notice. A statement by the Elementary Education Committee for Monmouthshire informed of what gifts the children would receive to mark the occasion. Good attendance generally rose in the local schools when it became known that the scholars would receive a designed Jubilee beaker and a special metal box containing chocolates.

Although suggested as one of the events for the Jubilee Day, ox roasting would not be included. So many complained about the barbaric practise that it would be confined to the history books in Torfaen. However, the chain of bonfires all over the country again appeared to be a popular activity and the boy scouts were to be the organisers. Some believed that with the general public by now conditioned to using a bus service, only few would take on the hard trek up to the Folly compared to the thousands in 1897. Workmen were given a day off with pay and the landlords of the district's hostelries, with much ado, eventually had extensions granted for Easter and Jubilee Day.

Samuel (Jack) Davies, Welsh Schoolboy Rugby International, 1935.

By the spring of 1935, it appeared that everyone wanted to participate in some way in the Jubilee celebrations. To arouse additional interest in the Pontypool Flower and Vegetable Show, specially struck Jubilee medals for the section winners became a success. A new competition at the Pontypool Golf Club saw the winner receive a handsome Jubilee silver bowl. In order to raise money for the King George's Trust Fund the game of rugby would make its contribution at all levels. Samuel (Jack) Davies, a Pentwyn schoolboy, had the honour of playing outside half for Wales against the England schoolboys in what was termed the Jubilee International. He would have a good game before later playing well for Pontypool R.F.C., while following a career in the police service. Pontypool's Jubilee match at home with Cardiff resulted in an entertaining game with a win for the city team. The specially organised game between Wales and the Rest would be far different. With key players dropping out, the game developed into a drab affair with Wales the eventual winners.

The amalgamation of the Pontypool, Abersychan and Panteg Councils took place in time for a concerted effort in the preparations for the important day.

Well-attended dances at the Town Hall and Palais-de-Danse raised funds for the King's fund whilst the Jubilee atmosphere saved one of the revellers. "I don't know what happened, something definitely went wrong with my legs," was the excuse of a 54-year-old labourer. Drunk in a Pontypool street, he had upset people going to church. Appearing in a special court on Jubilee morning, he said, "You can't do anything to me I am a 1914 man, and fought for my country." The magistrates would not convict on Jubilee Day, but advised the defendant to leave the district immediately.

Early morning rehearsals in the London streets indicated the great day was nearing. On May 6th, Jubilee Day, the King and Queen and members of the Royal family attended a Thanksgiving Service at St. Paul's Cathedral. In brilliant sunshine, and amidst a great roar of cheering, it was a never-to-be forgotten day for all those present at the roadside.

1935 - Princess Elizabeth with head resting on hands. No one on the balcony that day knew this small girl would sometime be Queen.

Cross, Pontypool, looking towards George Street, 1935.

George Street, Pontypool, 1935.

New Pontypool Council, 1935.

Council Chairman W.C. Watkins plants commerative oak tree in the Italian Gardens, 1935.

Jubilee Day in Torfaen would be truly remarkable.

In the lives of many Pontypool folk there had never been such a brightly coloured spectacle. Bunting, national flags, illuminations, flood lighting, beacons – all had their places in an ambitious scheme of celebration. George Street was a mass of streamers and flags, and side streets and outlying districts showed a huge dressing of colour. It was essentially a time for the elderly folk and the children. The new Pontypool Council had decided on the expenditure of a halfpenny on the rate, and out of this came gifts of two shillings to each blind and elderly person who was not in employment. For the schoolchildren a special tea would be eagerly consumed.

On Jubilee morning, members of the new Council joined others at a special service arranged by the Evangelical Council of Free Churches at St. David's Hall, Pontypool. After the service, Council Chairman, Alderman W.C. Watkins, of Victoria Village, planted an oak tree in the Italian Gardens to commemorate both the Silver Jubilee and the union of the Panteg, Abersychan and Pontypool Councils. (At a Council meeting on May 14th, 1935, it was resolved that a brass plate be fixed to the tree.)

Around eight thousand children sat down in the afternoon to a varied tea at their respective schools. The three Pontypool schools – George Street, Town School, and Park Terrace – assembled at each school and, carrying their own cups, marched to the beautifully decorated Market Hall to have a treat together. The Pontypool Town Voluntary School logbook tells of the following telegram of congratulations sent by the children to Their Majesties, as they tucked into all the good things:

"Fifteen hundred Pontypool schoolchildren send loyal greetings and hearty congratulations to Your Majesties."

A reply was received later in the day, which thrilled the children:

Buckingham Palace
Head Teacher,
"The King and Queen warmly thank the children of Pontypool for their kind Jubilee greetings.
Clive Wigram."

Entertaining Sports in the Park, with £20 allocated for prize money, followed the presentations of Jubilee beakers and boxes of chocolates for schools from Varteg to Panteg Wern School, Sebastopol.

Music in the Park by three bands - Pontypool Military Band, Pontypool Silver Band, and Varteg Band - in the evening, precluded the switching on of effective illuminations and flood lighting. The Town Hall became a blaze of colour when the

Sherbourne Road, Sebastopol, 1935.

Silver Jubilee party 1935 Sherbourne Road, Sebastopol.

Alexandra Road, Sebastopol, 1935.

South Street, Sebastopol, 1935.

38

switch was thrown in front of huge gathering of people of all ages. High up on the building was the beautifully illuminated Royal monogram, *"GR"* serving as the central emblem. On either side, the Prince of Wales feathers with hundreds of coloured lights added to the display. The Memorial Gates opposite had received a coat of varnish and the stonework an application of "Imstone" colouring, in readiness for the big day. The ornamental torches on either side of the main portal lit up for the first time. The Italian Gardens was a sight to behold. A large lamp in one of the trees flooded the fountain and ornamental lake with light and festoons of coloured lights in the trees made a particularly charming effect. The whole scene was greatly admired by many who sat or romantically strolled arm-in-arm around the gardens.

In the new urban area of Cwmbran the day began with a Thanksgiving Service in St. Gabriel's Church along the similar lines to that relayed from St. Paul's Cathedral. Following their Jubilee treats the children of St. Dial's, the Roman Catholic Schools and secondary school pupils, all headed to the Cwmbran Park behind the Cwmbran Brass Band. Here rustic sport was enjoyed with community singing in the evening.

At Blaenafon it would be an unforgettable scene. A great atmosphere of festivity prevailed. After the children received their treats, which included a Jubilee medal, all went to the Recreation Ground where everyone dressed in every colour of the rainbow. The lively programme for the afternoon and evening is still remembered by many in the popular little town. The town appears to have one distinction that was not publicized on the special day. The daughter of Mr. and Mrs Mogford, of Queen Street, was born in Blaenafon, on May 6th. In all probability Eileen Mary Mogford was the only child born on Jubilee Day in Torfaen. Three weeks later Eileen Mary, unknowingly, became the recipient of a handsome silver-christening cup in front of a large gathering. The cup, subscribed for by the Blaenafon Council, was presented by Miss May Lewis, the only lady member of the Council.

That evening, in Buckingham Palace, the King broadcast a message to the Empire that went from heart to heart. He said: -

"At the close of this memorable day I must speak to my people everywhere. Yet how can I express what is in my heart? As I passed this morning through cheering multitudes to and from St. Paul's Cathedral, as I thought there of all that these twenty five years have brought to me and to my country and my Empire, how could I failed to be most deeply moved? Words cannot express my thoughts or feelings. I can only say to you, my very dear people, that the Queen and I thank you from the very depth of our hearts for all the loyalty and – may I say? – the love with which this day and always you have surrounded us. I dedicate myself anew to your service for the years that may still be given to me.

The Commemoration of

Their Majesties' Silver Jubilee

... Celebrations Programme ...

MONDAY, MAY 6th, 1935.

THE BLAENAVON DISTRICT COUNCIL will provide tea for the Children attending the Elementary Schools in the places mentioned on the coloured tickets which will be distributed by the Head Teachers. Medals will be presented to all school children by the Councillors At Six o'clock a Procession will be formed at Cae White and will proceed via King Street, Broad Street, William Street, and Ton Mawr Road. to the Recreation Grounds.

ORDER OF PROCESSION.

1. Town Band.
2. The Volunteer Fire Brigade.
3. Members and Officials of the Council and County Council.
4. THE SCHOOL CHILDREN IN ORDER OF DATE OF SCHOOL.
   Church Endowed Schools.
   Park Street Schools.
   Roman Catholic Schools.
   Forge Side Schools.
   Garn-yr-erw Schools.
   Hillside Schools.
   NOTE—Scholars of Infants Schools are not expected to take part in the Procession.
5. The Workmen's Institute and Medical Society Committees.
6. The Chamber of Trade.
7. Representatives of Trade Unions.
8. Friendly Societies and the R.A.O.B.
9. The British Legion (Women's Section).
10. The British Legion.
11. Girl Guides.
12. Boy's Brigades and Boy Scouts.

The Officers and men of the Blaenavon Branch of the St. John's Ambulance Brigade will undertake the duties of Stewards.

The Parade will be under the direction of Mr. Chas. Pritchard, as Chief Marshal assisted by the Officers of the St. John's Ambulance.

ALL DECORATIONS TO BE WORN

The Head Teachers are kindly asked to undertake the marshalling of the children of their respective Schools.

A FIREWORKS DISPLAY

will be given at 9-0 p.m. in the Recreation Grounds. under the direction of Mr. T. J. BAKER
No persons will be allowed to enter the Grounds until after the procession has entered.

The Chairman of the Council, Councillor W. J. WATHEN, J. P. C. C. will light the bonfire at Penfforgoch at 9-55 p.m. prompt.

ALL TOWNSPEOPLE ARE ASKED TO DISPLAY FLAGS AND BUNTING ON JUBILEE DAY.

By ORDER OF THE BLAENAVON URBAN DISTRICT COUNCIL,

I. G. GWYN THOMAS,

Clerk to the Council.

"I look back on the past with thankfulness to God. My people and I have come through great trials and difficulties together. They are not over. In the midst of this day's rejoicing I grieve to think of the numbers of my people who are still without work. We owe to them, and not least to those who are suffering from any form of disablement, all the sympathy and help that we can give. I hope that during this Jubilee Year all who can will do their utmost to find them work and bring them hope.

"Other anxieties may be in store. But I am persuaded that with God's help they may all be overcome, if we meet them with confidence, courage, and unity. So I look forward to the future with faith and hope.

"It is to the young that the future belongs. I trust that through the Fund inaugurated by my dear son the Prince of Wales to commemorate this year many of them throughout this country may be helped in body, mind, and character to become useful citizens.

"To the children I would like to send a special message. Let me say this to each of them whom my words may reach: The King is speaking to you! I ask you to remember that in days to come you will be the citizens of a great Empire. As you grow up always keep this thought before you, and when the time comes be ready and proud to give to your country the service of your work, your mind, and your heart.

"I have been greatly touched by all your greetings which have come to me today from my Dominions and Colonies, from India and from this Home Country. My heart goes out to all who may be listening to me now wherever you may be – here at home in town or village, or in some far-off corner of the Empire, or may it be on the high seas.

"Let me end my words to you with those which Queen Victoria used after her Diamond Jubilee, thirty-eight years ago. No words could more truly or simply express my own deep feeling now: 'from my heart I thank my beloved people. May God bless them.'"

The Boy Scouts did a marvellous job organising the bonfires, which gave a fitting conclusion to a memorable day. Great care had been given to the building of the large beacons and also to protecting the sites from anyone with mischievous intentions who wanted a preview of the celebratory event.

The 1st Varteg Boy's Brigade erected a large bonfire on the Mine Tips, Varteg, with material supplied by Messrs John Vipond and Co. Ltd. After the hundreds present had sung "God Save the Queen", Miss Jessamine Davies had the honour of lighting the beacon. Community singing lasted well into the night.

The Abersychan troop of scouts worked hard carrying combustible material up the steep Pantglas mountainside. On the evening a signal rocket gave Alderman W.C. Watkins notice to light the bonfire and within minutes the whole area was lit up and community singing commenced.

The Lower Valley Boy Scouts forged their link in the chain of beacons in celebration with a splendid display on Cwmlicky Mountain, Penyrheol. Hundreds gathered for a singsong led by the scouts.

At the Folly a huge bonfire burned magnificently for the many who had caught the bus to Trevethin Church and then relied on Shank's pony to reach the spot. The celebrations would continue to the early hours of Tuesday morning.

Silver Jubilee events would continue throughout the summer months giving pleasure to many. At the beginning of July the Pontypool Hospital Fete and Carnival continued in the same theme. Good weather would attract large crowds, which boosted the much-needed funds required by the hospital. On children's day, a thirteen-year-old Newport girl, Joan Griffin, was chosen as the *South Wales Argus* Queen Titania. Mrs G.E. Didbin, wife of the manager of the *South Wales Argus* newspaper, crowned the charming young lady with a silver crown. The next day, and in front of a large crowd, Mrs Leonora Hough, the mannequin wife of a London artist made her entry as Miss Jubilee. Her court ladies were five previous Pontypool fete winners and included Mrs Vera David (Miss Eva Coombes) 1929, Talywain, and Miss Dorothy Booth, Pontypool, 1932. For the special year, Miss. Gladys E. Stone, of Broadway, Pontypool, represented Britannia, and held a position of prominence behind Miss Jubilee during the parade. It would prove to be an interesting crowning ceremony. Chosen to do the honour was a famous film star, Miss Jean Adrieene, who had just appeared in a leading role in the film "The Broken Rosary." A few months after her Pontypool visit she also appeared in the leading film role of "Barnacle Bill," which enticed many Torfaen folk to visit the Pavilion Cinema at Pontnewynydd.

43

Sandbrook and Dawe Ltd, Pontypool, 1935.

A new medal, known as the King's Jubilee Medal, appeared and was regarded as a personal souvenir from His Majesty. It would be awarded in recognition of service during his reign by selecting members of the Crown and other services. The following are known recipients:

Mrs Dora Nelms, 37, Wainfelin Avenue, Pontypool. – Ambulance worker.
Mr. W.H.V. Bythway, clerk to the Pontypool Council.
Mr. I.G. Gwyn Thomas, clerk to the Blaenafon Council.
Alderman W.C. Watkins, J.P., chairman of the Pontypool Urban District Council.
Mr. W.J. Wathen, J.P., chairman of Blaenafon Council.
Mr. John Morgan, rating office to Blaenafon Council.
Mr. E.L. Parker, J.P., chairman of Pontypool R.D.C.
Mr. E.A. Pryer, chairman of Cwmbran Council.
Mr. William Clark, clerk to Cwmbran Council.
Superintendent Laurence Spendlove.
Police Sergeant Gordon Jones, Cwmbran.
Superintendent Walbyoff, M.B.E., Pontypool.
Mr. J.L. Smith, Pontypool Post Office.
Mr. W.T. Truman, Pontypool Fire Brigade.

Film star Jean Adrieene crowns 1935 Silver Jubilee Queen

1935 Silver Jubilee Queen joins the parade.

"Titania" 13 year old Joan Griffin, 1935 Jubilee Fete.

Mary Rogers, a young Jubilee Queen at Victoria Village May Festival.

Major Harold Griffiths, Griffithstown, receives O.B.E. in birthday honours list, 1935.

Torfaen would be well represented in the Honours List issued on the King's birthday. Mr. Emmanuel Barson, J.P., of Blaenafon, received the Order of the British Empire for his active public work over a long period. Major Harold Griffiths, of St. Dunstan's, Griffithstown, also received the O.B.E. The son of the founder of the delightful town, Major Griffiths had received the King's Jubilee Medal only a short time before. As a young man he joined the Imperial Yeomanry and served his country well in the Boer War. For many years he had been involved in the Cadet movement and held the rank of Colonel Commandant at the time of the Silver Jubilee. As a man of many activities, he thoroughly deserved his unexpected second award.

It had been a wonderful time for everyone throughout the country. King George V was indeed a quiet, family man and disciplined to carrying out his duty. He proved a very popular king – just how popular he himself didn't realise until he'd driven through London's East End streets and saw them bedecked with Union Jacks and lined with cloth capped workers who ran after his Daimler shouting good luck messages. " I'd no idea they felt like that about me," he remarked as he arrived back at Buckingham Palace. "I am beginning to think they must really like me for myself."

Jubilee Day Ceremony at Trevethin Church. Silver Jubilee gift of new gates replace previous gates dedicated in 1887, the year of Queen Victoria's Golden Jubilee.

Chapter Four

The NINETEEN-FIFTIES

To many the nineteen-fifties was a magical time. Life began to change dramatically as Britain entered a modern era. The effects of the World War Two still existed, but gradually things were changing for the better. The war had plunged Britain into debt slowing down the clearing of bombsites and rubble before new houses could be built. Food had been short and ration books allowed only the purchase of a measured amount of goods each week. Clothes, petrol and soap were in short supply, however, children under five years old were allowed extra orange juice and cod-liver oil.

During the early nineteen-fifties things vastly improved. Clothes, meat, milk and eggs became more plentiful. By 1953, children could at last buy as many sweets as they liked from the corner shop. The following year rationing ended completely and the psychological depression of the people began to lift. However, in order to keep the army, navy and air force strong, National Service had been introduced. Every young man had to spend two years in the service of his country when he reached the age of eighteen years. This commitment would only last until the end of the fifties. Many would fight in the Korean War between 1950 and 1955, and anxieties of parents of a new generation would emerge. Far from the scale of conflict of the world war a decade previously, the young men of Torfaen would play their part and sadly three would die for their country:

    Captain   H.B. Evans – The British Army Corps of Royal Engineers
    Corporal G. Leonard – Northumberland Fusiliers
    Corporal Frederick Henry Meech – The Welch Regiment

There would be some happier stories from that distant land. Two Garndiffaith lads met in Korea. Rifleman Albert Rogers met up with Corporal T.R. Casey of the 7th Royal Tank Regiment and agreed to meet in their local when they arrived home. Graham Williams, of Blaenafon, wounded while serving with the 1st Welch Regiment recovered and returned home. Private Kenneth C. Williams, of Cwmbran, also with the Welch Regiment, met another Cwmbran man Keith Howard, before receiving a disabling gunshot wound. For the relatives of Kingsmen Brynley Jones, Pontypool, and Barry Roberts, Pontnewydd, it would be a time for celebration. After wrongly being reported as "killed" they returned to their units after five weeks in hospital with gunshot wounds. Alas, there would be no let up from the threat of war. The possibility of conflict between the United States and Russia brought about the beginning of the Cold War, in which nuclear weapons might be used.

People's homes hadn't changed much since Victorian times. Many were terraced houses with outside toilets and no bathrooms, and were often damp and badly heated. In Trosnant, an old part of Pontypool, the houses were very much worn out and described as hovels. The Council would soon condemn many of them. Conditions changed with housing estates springing up everywhere. By 1950 a plan was underway to build a new town on the Cwmbran site complete with all the conveniences for modern living. Planned originally to house a population of 35,000 over the following fifteen years, the number would be far in excess of this by the completion of the huge project. Understandably, many young married couples would leave the upper reaches of Torfaen to take advantage of the new style of living. Fortunately, the new town would have only one high-rise block of flats. These buildings were popular at first, but soon found to be depressing and often dangerous for children. However, the tall building would serve well as a landmark for the new, landscaped town.

In spite of the building boom, many people were still homeless. As a stopgap, some Torfaen folk were allocated a quickly erected bungalow type home known as a prefab. This arrangement, complete with a refrigerator, became the envy of many. Built to last only ten years, some prefabs are still being lived in today!

Gadgets were soon to open up a new way of life for the housewife. New inventions like the washing machine, took much of the effort out of housework, leaving more free time for other pursuits. The refrigerator, while keeping food fresh, made frequent journeys to the shops unnecessary. However, until frozen foods became widely available in the mid-fifties, only about three per cent of the population owned a fridge. Hot water could miraculously be drawn straight from the kitchen tap and no longer had to be warmed up on a stove. The vacuum cleaner immediately became the housewife's choice by taking much of the drudgery out of housework. These items could be bought on hire purchase, or the 'never-never.' This allowed for the cost to be paid off, bit by bit, over a period of time. Today, the use of all these machines are regarded as the expected way of living, but to the people of the fifties it was a whole new world opening for them.

Other new ideas made houses easier to manage. Stainless steel sinks and plastic bowls could be wiped instead of scrubbed as enamel and tin had to be. Powerful washing powders and disinfectants were advertised, encouraging people to keep kitchens and bathrooms free of dirt. Furniture styles changed just as quickly. New man-made fibres replaced the drab furnishings people had become so familiar with.

At the start of the fifties shopping, for many people, meant going to the small grocery shop usually at the end of a road. There they could buy nearly everything they needed, from vegetables and jam to newspapers and paraffin. Apart from a few tins, jars and cartons of cereals, there were few packaged foods. Bacon and cheeses were cut to order, and salt was sold in large blocks. Grocery shops gave a personal service to customers and the value of goods seems quite unlike the cost of things today. Many folk will still remember, when as children, taking a grocery list to the corner shop, and collecting food items for which their mothers would pay at the end of the week. In those far off days the coinage was so different. Instead of the pounds we have now, with each containing one hundred pence, the currency in the fifties consisted of a pound containing twenty shillings. A guinea was twenty-one shillings. Each shilling was made up of twelve old pennies with the letter d indicating how many pennies were accounted for.

In 1954, an average family with two children spent nearly three pounds each week on food. This might not seem much today, but in the typical family only the father worked and his weekly earnings would not have been more than about ten pounds. Weekly rent for a three-bedroom semi-detached house was between three and four pounds. Although rationing was over, people's meals still lacked variety. The wage earner often had a manual job and subsequently his plate would be piled high with fatty foods and stodgy puddings. These recipes unfortunately, would continue when the need for a lot of calories was no longer required for energy. The range of foods newly available became more obvious to people with the advent of the supermarket. More than six hundred self-service shops opened in 1956 alone. Many of them offered a wider choice than the corner shops, and at the time was an exciting new experience for the shopper. This was to be the start of the smaller shops going out of business and high streets everywhere began to look depressingly alike.

It was easy to find work during the fifties. After the Second World War, British industry re-established itself quickly, and soon only one per cent of those looking for work were unemployed. Young men were still expected to go into local industries, while some broke away from the mundane work they were expected to carry out for their lifetimes and sought more exciting work and careers further afield. Some chose to work in newly built factories. The work was lighter and far cleaner than the steelworks or the pit, and the machines much safer to use. Working hours were longer than today's, and holidays were shorter – two weeks instead of the long breaks we expect now.

On farms, machines began to take over many of the difficult tasks previously done by men or horses. Tractors were used to haul ploughs and harrows, and the first combine harvesters appeared in the Torfaen fields. This caused a dramatic fall in the total number of people employed on the land.

*Arthur Jones of Ty-Ambrose Farm, a rare sight in the 1950's
with Panteg steelworks in the background.*

However, for the first time workers did not fear poverty if they were ill or out of a job. Every week they and their employers had to contribute to the National Insurance Scheme, which had been set up in 1948. This made sure that they would receive regular sums of money when they retired, or when they were sick or unemployed.

Just after the war, there was a 'baby boom.' Many of the couples parted by war wanted to start families so the birth rate shot up. By the fifties, the children of that boom were ready to go to school. Many new schools had to be built for them. These were roomier and better equipped than the old schools, but it took a long time for them all to be completed. Meanwhile, many children had to make do with wooden huts for classrooms.

Children went to primary school at the age of five. They sat at their own desks and some would use pens with detachable nibs, provided by the school, to learn to write. Others would bring fountain pens to school, which made their writing much cleaner and the use of blotting paper less likely. Discipline was far stricter than it is today, and a child would be beaten with a cane. School's punishment books, now deposited in County Record Offices all over the country for safekeeping, witness this. One former Torfaen schoolboy remembers receiving six of the best for a minor infringement. His headmaster was a tall man and not only was it a form of torture waiting for the cane to travel the long way down to his hand, but he was sure there was ice on it when it arrived. His comment was that he made sure he never received the punishment a second time.

The 1944 Education Act made school attendance compulsory up to the age of fifteen, and at the age of eleven, children sat an examination called the 'eleven plus.' This examination would decide if a child went to a grammar school or a secondary modern school. Many parents were worried that eleven years old was too young to measure a child's potential and that if their children went to a secondary modern school, there was less chance of them gaining a highly paid executive job afterwards. At the end of the decade the government tried to resolve this problem by introducing a new type of school – the comprehensive. Because of this they could offer a much wider range of subjects and allow each child to develop at his or her own pace.

The call went out for a healthier land and the health situation improved immensely. During the fifties more care was taken over the health of each member of the family, especially the children. Most babies were born in hospital, and fewer died at birth. They were vaccinated at an early age to protect them against terrible diseases such as polio and tuberculosis. People in Britain were also becoming taller and heavier. Better food, and more of it, strengthened their bones and built them up. Doctors now understood how vitamins and protein could help growing children. They also had stronger medicines with which to cure illness. The new National Health Service had been set up in 1948, providing free treatment by doctors, dentists and opticians. Later, the government brought back charges for prescriptions and spectacles, but this proved very unpopular. Some hospitals found it hard to cope. Many of them were cramped and old-fashioned and did not have enough beds for the patients. However, hospitals at Blaenafon, Pontnewynydd and Panteg served their communities well during this period and a small convalescent hospital at Snatchwood enhanced the warm, caring feeling all these units gave to the people of the eastern valley.

People began to take leisure time more seriously. Getting about was much easier in Torfaen with good rail and bus services. Gradually more cars were introduced to the district and children were not seen to be playing their games in the streets as before. Many would take advantage of the excursions to the seaside. Barry Island would be a popular railway excursion. At this time leisurewear was not widely worn and many Torfaen men snoozed on the beach in heavy suits and a knotted handkerchief on their heads to protect from the sun's rays.

Air travel had always proved too expensive yet some took advantage of the short flight to Ireland to watch a rugby international match. A disaster, which shook not only Torfaen, but also the whole of Wales, occurred on March 12th, 1950. Eighty lives were lost when an aeroplane full of rugby supporters crashed at Llandow. Among the casualties was former Squadron Leader Bill Irvine, D.F.C., of Griffithstown. A stain glassed window, which served as his memorial was later presented to St. Hilda's Church by The Mothers' Union. By the mid-fifties cheap tourist flights were introduced to Spain and France. A week's holiday in Paris, including the hotel bill, could cost as little as twenty-four pounds. In spite of the cheap airfares, most families spent their holidays in Britain. Many factories and mines shut down during August, and thousands of people flocked to the seaside. It was said that a place on the Porthcawl beach became impossible to find during the miner's annual two-week holiday. For those who liked holidays to be highly organised, there were the holiday camps. These became hugely popular during this period, because they offered swimming pools, children's playgrounds, competitions and nighttime shows.

Unknown to everyone the Festival of Britain in 1951 would in many ways be a trial run for the coronation of Queen Elizabeth II, a few years later. To celebrate one hundred years of British enterprise a wonderful exhibition of past and modern technology appeared in London. The whole country would participate by organising interesting events. Torfaen was not slow in joining in. Flags, bunting and street parties could be seen everywhere. It was a wonderful week for the Torfaen children with a variety of events organised by the Pontypool Council in the park. Festival Week in Pontypool demonstrated without a doubt the wonderful community spirit, which had always been part of life in the valley.

Beer consumption rose dramatically. Every weekend enormous crowds watched cricket, football and other sporting events. Several achievements caught the public imagination: Roger Bannister became the first man to run a four-minute mile; Jim Laker took a record nineteen wickets in a cricket match against Australia. Throughout Torfaen, children tried to emulate their sporting heroes.

Perhaps the biggest change of all in family life was caused by television, or 'the box', as it was often called. Many people bought their first set in 1953 so that they could watch the coronation. This new entertainment caused a young Torfaen resident to increase his pocket money when he regularly charged his chums one penny to view a programme of their choice. Television sets in those days were comparatively expensive. They had small screens – as narrow as twenty centimetres across – and sometimes folded doors, which were closed when the set was turned off. There were no colour pictures – only black and white. In time this new, easy entertainment, had other effects. Although there was a possibility of learning from the media, many Torfaen children spent less time playing out of doors, talking to each other, or discovering things for themselves.

By the end of the fifties, Britain had become a prosperous society, with plenty of money to spend. Adults spent theirs on mortgages or rent, holidays and gadgets for the home. Youngsters leaving school easily found a job with many of them earning good wages. These young people had money to spend on themselves and even the schoolchildren had a larger allowance. Entrepreneurs were already providing a market for what was recognised as a teenage revolution. For the first time, fashionable clothes were in the shops for young people. Girls wore wide skirts with stiff petticoats and shoes with thin 'stiletto' heels. Some had their hair brushed up in a style called a 'beehive', and most wore makeup.

Boys' fashions changed even more. Jeans and woollen jumpers became popular. The wilder 'Teddy boys' (so called because their clothes were like Edwardian fashions) dressed themselves in skin-tight trousers, long coats and boot-string ties. On their feet were pointed 'winkle-pecker' shoes. Torfaen would see its fair share of angry young men during this period. On Sundays, after church, for some time a ritual occurred when boys and girls, dressed in the latest fashion, would continuously parade from one end of the Pontypool shopping area to the other, and then back again. Boy would meet girl and many met their future husbands or wives. Dressed in the latest style, teenagers were ready for a night out. Most were too young to go into pubs, which were rather quiet and dull. Instead they sat in coffee bars, or milk parlours, where they drank frothy coffee, a milkshake or a fizzy drink. The latest pop records could be selected by putting money into a jukebox, and another diversion was playing the slot machines, or 'one-armed bandits', with pennies and sixpenny pieces. On Saturday nights, teenagers went to the local dance hall. In the early fifties dance halls only allowed old-fashioned dances such as the two-step. Soon everyone wanted to jive (a lively, hip swinging dance to rock-'n'-roll music), and the rock-'n'-roll era was created.

The pop music explosion had begun in earnest with young people trying to learn to play the guitar and dreaming of finding fame with a recorded song, even if it would only be for a short time. Only a few would make it to the top. Torfaen had the unusual distinction of having a young girl reach the dizzy heights of the pop world. Jean Callow, of Sebastopol, and her cousin Vann Jenkins, of Hereford, formed a successful singing partnership as the Terry Sisters. They would appear regularly on the radio and television and the fierce competition everywhere at the time for musical fame seems to have diminished the unique achievement of a girl from our midst.

It was said that trout would be seen again in the Afon Lwyd by the end of the fifties, but folk had to wait a while longer for that to happen. Life went on and as a fitting end to wonderful fifties, the popular newspaper; *The Free Press of Monmouthshire* reached its 100th milestone in 1959. Following a telegram of loyal greetings from the staff to our beautiful young queen, a message of congratulations was received from Her Majesty.

Chapter Five

THE CORONATION

Princess Elizabeth was only twenty-five years old when her father died. She had been married for just over four years and she and her naval husband were enjoying bringing up their two small children, Charles and Anne. But now, with the sudden death of King George VI, Elizabeth was Queen.

Few people outside the Royal Family had known how ill the King was. In March 1949 he had undergone an operation to improve the circulation in his right foot. In 1951 it was confirmed he had a growth in his left lung but, after an operation, he seemed to have made such a good recovery that plans were organised for a holiday in South Africa the following March.

Princess Elizabeth and Prince Philip were due to leave on a tour of East Africa, Australia and New Zealand on the last day of January 1952 and, the night before they left, the King felt well enough to take his family to see the musical *South Pacific* at London's Drury Lane.

But the following day was cold and bleak, with a biting wind, and people were shocked to see the newspaper pictures showing how gaunt and ill the King looked as he waved his daughter and son-in-law goodbye at London Airport.

Five days later King George was at Sandringham and enjoying a day's rough shooting, tramping over frost-crusted earth for nearly six hours. He came home to join the Queen and their grandchildren for tea in the nursery, and after dinner listened to the news on the wireless about Princess Elizabeth's tour. He retired to his bedroom on the ground floor about 10.30 p.m., read a magazine, and drank a cup of cocoa. At 7.30 a.m. the following morning one of his valets entered the room, drew back the curtains, and found that the King had died in his sleep. The cause was coronary thrombosis. His age was fifty-six years.

Prince Philip broke the news to his wife. They had spent the night in a small observation house, now called Treetops, in the Aberdare Forest of Kenya watching and filming wildlife. By the following afternoon when a news agency report had been officially confirmed, they went back to the royal hunting lodge at Sagana, where they had been spending a few days holiday.

Immediately, arrangements were made for the new Queen to fly to Entebbe, and then on through that night and the next day to London. Her plane landed at London Airport on an evening of drizzly darkness. As she came down the steps, in black and totally alone, her senior ministers of Government bowed, bareheaded, in grief and

*King George VI and Queen Elizabeth arriving at Pontypool Road Station,
10th December 1941.*

*King George VI and Queen Elizabeth wartime visit to Town Forge, Pontypool,
10th December 1941.*

homage. It seemed that night, as though the whole of the nation were stilled, as in prayer. Almost 400 years after Elizabeth I, a second Elizabeth had acceded to the Throne of England, and under the sadness lay hope that a new, golden age might soon begin.

By midmorning on February 6th, 1952, the people of the eastern valley knew their King had passed away. This brave and popular man had won the respect of a nation and would be truly mourned. Called to his duty so suddenly and in painful circumstances, he assumed the heavy responsibilities of kingship without flinching, and carried them out successfully to the end of his life. Many local folk would remember the day in December 1941, when he and his wife arrived at Pontypool Road Station to be met by Lord Raglan, Lord Lieutenant of Monmouthshire, prior to a visit to Pontypool Town Forge Tinplate Works. The exciting occasion cheered up the local inhabitants who, like everyone at the time, were feeling the cruel effects of a world war.

Immediately local authorities and the courts went into recess and Mr. L.C. Lewis, chairman of the Pontypool Council, sent the following telegram on behalf of the authority:

"HM The Queen, Sandringham, Norfolk. – It is with profound sorrow that the people of Pontypool have learned of the sudden death of our beloved Sovereign, and I am to convey their deepest sympathies to Your Majesty and the other members of the Royal Family".

The Griffithstown School logbook recorded the following:

February 6th. We have been shocked today to hear of the sudden passing of His Majesty the King. We all feel a keen sense of personal loss.

February 7th. Special prayers this morning during which the Head Teacher spoke of the great Christian character of the late King and children and teachers stood with bowed heads in silent sympathy with the Royal Family.

February 11th. This week the scripture readings will be in keeping with the week's mourning.

Minutes of a meeting of the Cwmbran Urban District Council record:

The Chairman of the Council referred with deep regret to the death of King George VI on 6th February 1952, and stated that he knew members would wish to record their deep sympathy with the new Queen and members of her family. The Clerk reported that a telegram had been despatched to Queen Elizabeth conveying the sincere sympathy of the residents of the Urban Area, and that the telegram had been suitably acknowledged. It was resolved that time off be allowed to all members of the staff to attend the Memorial Service to be held on 15 February 1952.

The gloom of the nation's bereavement was lifted for a few hours on the morning of Friday, February 8th, 1952. At 11 a.m., on that historic day, Elizabeth was proclaimed Queen in London and the cities, towns and villages throughout the land.

The following entry in the popular and loyal *Free Press of Monmouthshire* newspaper records for all time the proceedings on that momentous day:

'Thousands gathered at Blaenavon, Pontypool and Cwmbran to hear the Proclamation read from the council offices. At Pontypool all traffic in Hanbury Road was brought to a halt for ten minutes while Mr. Lothian C. Lewis, JP, chairman of the Council, read the Proclamation from the steps of the Town Hall to the crowd who had gathered in the road. Buses were left while drivers, conductors and passengers joined the crowd and sang "God Save the Queen". Among the council group was Mr. Charles Newman who last sang "God Save the Queen" during the reign of Victoria, while he was serving as a regular soldier with the Rifle Brigade.

'It was a memorable day for the schoolchildren, who gathered in hundreds to hail the new Queen. They formed a large part of the crowd in Lion Street, Blaenavon, where Councillor Sidney Banks, chairman of the Council, read the Proclamation, and at Cwmbran, where it was read by the Rev. John Donne, chairman of the Council and vicar at Llantarnam.

Among the crowd at Pontypool were some fifty-five children from Abersychan Mixed School who arrived in a char-a-banc. Only the senior classes and teachers of the Pontypool Town School attended, while the remainder of the school heard the Proclamation Ceremony, on the wireless, from London and Cardiff.

On February 15th, 1952, the London crowds gathered quietly for the funeral of King George VI. The whole of the Eastern Valley joined the nation's mourning. It was the wish of Queen Elizabeth that a nationwide two minutes' silence should commence at 2 p.m. on the day. In Pontypool, at 2 p.m., a large crowd stood bareheaded outside the Town Hall and all the traffic drew to a standstill. In local schools the two minutes silence was solemnly observed and at the Pontypool Town School Infant's Department the children listened to the radio broadcast of the funeral procession. Religious services were well attended throughout the districts and at the Trinity Methodist Church, Abersychan, Rev. F. Wilcox closed his address with a fitting tribute that was echoed by everyone present:

"The human qualities, the kingly virtues and pre-eminently, the spiritual qualities of our late King George VI supply the reason why all people today share in such deep, universal sorrow. We pay homage to our late King for whom it could be said: 'the sunset of his death has tinged the whole world's sky'."

After a respectful period of time passed for mourning, the months of preparation for the coronation of Queen Elizabeth II began. Pontypool got off to an early start with the opening of the lavish Queen's Ballroom on November 18th, 1952. It was the brainchild of T.H. Powell, a local businessman who bought the old worn out Palais-de-Danse and gave the interior of the building the breathtaking appearance of a palace. Not an inside ornamental wall was untouched with mirrors everywhere, and the elegant arched roof artistically re-painted. Named in honour of the new Queen, her royal portrait mounted on a large plaque in the dance hall was unveiled in front of a large gathering.

Coronation Year began with no outward interest of the amazing event, which would take place on June 2nd. However, behind the scenes, appropriate bodies had started to make their plans and a significant celebration began to take shape. Quite rightly the Pontypool Licensed Victuallers' Association campaigned early for Sunday opening of public houses during June as part of the Coronation festivities. Alas, luck was against Mr. W.R. Dadge, the Pontypool Parks superintendent, when all his planting for a special celebratory floral display was utterly destroyed by sheep roaming in the park. The members of New Inn Coronation Committee also had problems and appeared aggrieved enough to ask the Council for a road sweep to prepare the road in readiness for their party.

Despite the sad death in March of Queen Mary, wife of King George V, and grandmother to the Queen about to be crowned, preparations for the forthcoming historic day began to take on a new urgency.

The Whitsun Fete in Pontypool Park on Monday and Tuesday was blessed with what many described as a heat wave. Organised in support of the Senior Citizen's Christmas Fund, the event became a huge success. At first its promoters believed that their gate receipts would be badly reduced by the decision of many local industries to work over the holiday so that time could be taken off to celebrate the Coronation. They had no need to worry because the housewives, taking full advantage of the heat wave, put on their cool summer frocks and with excited children, arrived in force.

The highlight of Monday's events was the crowning of eighteen-year-old Maureen Sullivan, of Lowlands Crescent, Pontnewydd, as Pontypool's Coronation Beauty Queen. Dark haired Maureen, a sixth-form student at Pontypool Girls' County School, made a charming picture, accompanied by her entourage, on the open dais decorated in the patriotic colours of red, white and blue. Later in the afternoon the Coronation Queen visited Pontypool and Panteg Hospitals and spoke to all the patients. In the evening the young ladies attended a dance in the splendid new Queen's Ballroom.

Lieutenant-Colonel Harry Llewellyn, who captained the British horse jumping team in the Olympic Games at Helsinki in 1951, thrilled another big crowd at the Park by taking part in the customary Whit-Tuesday horse show and gymkhana. On this occasion he rode Master Deisel in the Grade A jumping competition, and was one of three riders who completed a clear round.

Looked upon by many as a Coronation present to the new Queen, the highest mountain in the world was finally climbed by a team on 29 May 1953. The team, with British leader Colonel John Hunt, had followed a route not tried before for the summit of Everest to be reached by New Zealander Edmund Hillary and Sherpa guide Tensing. A remarkable fact emerged that the nylon equipment used on the expedition was produced at the British Nylon Spinners factory at Pontypool. On 16 June, knighthoods would be conferred on Colonel Hunt and Edmund Hillary and the George Medal on Sherpa Tensing. A few months' later Torfaen schoolchildren would be walked to their local cinemas to view the epic adventure.

Elizabeth was at last to be crowned Queen. After sixteen months of detailed planning everything was ready for the greatest celebration known to the modern world. It had been sixteen years since the last coronation and the young Queen insisted on a few improvements to the existing plan. With the help of Prince Philip, the length of the route was increased to allow the many thousands of children to see the procession. A suggestion by the Coronation Commission that the event should not be televised was soon dropped, much to the relief of village organisers who would temporarily install as many as three borrowed sets in the local hall. The Imperial State Gown had to be remodelled for the Queen and the magnificent State Coach built for George III in 1761, in which she would to travel to and from Westminster Abbey, was renovated and re-gilded.

Hundreds of thousands of people thronged the streets of London to cheer the procession between Westminster Abbey and Buckingham Palace. It proved to be a wet June and although some were soaked through it did not deter them from vociferously cheering the great procession.

The procession would consist of five sections and the whole would take over four hours to pass a given point. Taking part in the procession was Guardsman Bernard Harris, aged 19 years, of the 1st Battalion, Welsh Guards. On leave, he would arrive home to 41, Penylan Road, Varteg, and here it was made known that although so young he had also marched in Queen Mary's funeral procession and taken part in the Trooping of the Colour. Another tough, but interesting duty was undertaken by Naval Airman Graham Wyatt, of Granville House, Osborne Road, Pontypool. He was on duty on the Coronation route and had a grand view of the proceedings. Lance Corporal Arthur Reynolds, Royal Engineers, of Pentrepiod, did similar duty and to assist with medical emergencies, representatives from Torfaen were on standby. Chosen from the Pontypool and District St. John Ambulance Corps for duty near the War Office in Whitehall were Mrs G.M. Thomas (Pontnewynydd Division), Mr. C.J. Powell (Pontypool), Mr. V.A. Collier (Griffithstown), Mr. R.T. Lawrence and Cadets A.P. Strike and C. Poulton (Pontnewydd).

Among the eight bandsmen who had the exacting task of sounding the trumpet fanfares in the Westminster Abbey procession was Student Bandmaster G.E. Evans, of the Royal Military School of Music. He was the son of Mr and Mrs W. Evans, South Street, Sebastopol, and worked in the boot department of Pontypool Co-operative store before joining the army. Also present in the Abbey on that remarkable occasion was the son of a Pentwyn schoolteacher. David Lewis, of Leigh Road, Pontypool, was a member of St. Paul's Cathedral Choir and would sing during the historic ceremony. Fourteen year-old David had been a member of Trevethin Church choir before winning a scholarship to St. Paul's five years previously.

Over two hours had passed and the Crown was placed on the head of a brave young women. In a nearby gallery a young boy, who was not on the official guest list, watched his mother being crowned Queen while he sometimes asked his grandmother questions and burrowed into her handbag looking for sweets. Everyone stood and shouted "God Save the Queen", and the trumpets sounded. The guns fired at the Tower of London and the people knew they had a new Monarch.

In Torfaen the great day had at last arrived and brought with it a community spirit found to be evident everywhere. Schoolchildren were on holiday. Some had parties before they broke up and received their Coronation souvenir. For the younger children a beaker with the portrait of their new Queen and a tin of chocolates were proudly carried home. The children over twelve years-of-age received a Coronation spoon. It would be a Coronation bonus of 5/- for the senior citizens, with instructions to pick it up in the same way as they collected their Xmas money. Some, with too much dignity, would not accept the gift.

The people of Pontypool, as always, did the town proud with its brightly coloured streets showing a practical demonstration of loyalty and patriotism. The profuse regalia provided by the Pontypool Council on the Town Hall and Clarence Street caused many a young child to gaze in wonderment. No effort had been spared in the Park with focal points adorned with flower boxes, hanging boxes and special gardens, which radiated an array of beautiful colours. Except for a short downpour in the

afternoon, which caused folk to abandon the streets and quickly head for halls, chapels and schoolrooms, the fun was non-stop. A fete in the Park gave extra entertainment when an exciting and varied programme of events met with almost continuous cheering. To enter into the spirit of the occasion the Council purchased over 6,000 souvenir crown brooches, pins, pennants and Union Jacks to present to the children who used the four entrances to the Park. Limitless sideshows and extra attractions kept the children occupied while the Tea Garden, opened especially for Coronation Week, did a roaring trade with their parents. A model passenger railway train operated on the putting green by Mr. F. Wilson, of Sebastopol, proved to be the most popular attraction with children and adults. On their tour of the Park, people would stop and admire the recently planted Coronation tree and commemorative seat placed on a piece of ground on the Convent side of the bandstand. Fireworks and dancing in the floodlit park ring officially ended a wonderful day.

There would be no lack of enthusiasm for Coronation Week in Blaenafon. All of the town's chief buildings were floodlit and every colliery in the area also provided floodlighting with a Union Jack hoisted in good view. June 2nd was undoubtedly children's day with many receiving the coveted crown pieces. Everyone entered the carnival spirit. Streets competed with each other for the prizes offered by the Council for the best decorated. All efforts were appreciated; even those of the elderly lone widows who could only managed a newspaper cutting in their front room windows. A huge tea soon vanished when the children tucked in as circulating councillors distributed a magnificent souvenir to one and all. This proved to be a brochure of historical interest and still remains a treasured keepsake of that happy time all those years ago. Two Blaenafon ladies had an even busier time on Coronation Day producing additions to their families. They were:

Mrs Mattie Hill, wife of Archie Hill, of 6, Cwmavon Road, Blaenafon. A son born 12.15 a.m., in Crickhowell Hospital.

Mrs Betty Parry, of Capel Newydd Avenue, Blaenafon, a daughter Gail, at 8.20 p.m., born in Panteg Hospital. Both mothers were inundated with Coronation gifts. While all the babies born before the special day at Panteg Hospital received a Coronation spoon from the nursing staff, Mrs Parry was presented with a beautiful maternity coat for her baby. Proof that she was not forgotten in Blaenafon occurred when a souvenir cup and saucer arrived from the caring residents of her street.

Cwmbran commenced its Coronation Week with a splendid carnival and fete. A huge procession toured Cwmbran village and the new town before arriving at Grange Road Sports Field. Here, proceedings began with the formal opening by the chairman of Cwmbran Council, Mr. Frederick J. Gifford, whose wife crowned the Coronation

"Coronation Day"

BY ANN REDDEN—St. Dial's Girls' School
(Aged 13 years, 10 months)

Through London's crowded streets to-day
  Our lovely Queen will ride,
'Mid merry shouts and happy cheers,
  Prince Philip at her side.

No Queen was ever loved so much
  As she we'll crown to-day,
And we, her loyal subjects, shall
  Have each our part to play.

In capital, town and hamlet,
  And lands beyond the sea,
The people all will celebrate,
  And praise Her Majesty.

And two little royal children
  Will gaze upon the throng,
With hearts so full of wonderment,
  And on their lips a song.

O, beautiful Queen and mother,
  O, loyal heart and true,
We pray God will be with you
  For all life's journey through.

Left to right: Pat Strawford, Marilyn Samuel (Junior Floral Queen),
Gabrielle Willis Cwmbran Coronation Queen, Sybil Tonks

queen, beautiful blue-eyed Gabrielle Willis, of Victoria Street, Cwmbran. Her court
ladies were Marion Tremeer, Molly Powell, Patricia Strawford, and Sybil Tonks, all of
Cwmbran. On another tableau was the junior floral queen, 12-year-old Marilyn
Samuel, of Croesyceiliog, whose attendants were sisters Jill and Jane Honing, Marilyn
Fry, Anita Strawford, Sandra Sheppard and Linda Carpenter. A fun week included
parties, dances, competitions for the best-decorated street, and on the great day the
elderly folk watched the Coronation proceedings on televisions temporary installed in
the Cwmbran Catholic Hall. At dusk on this special day a scout group lighted a
beacon on the mountain.

The year would produce an abundance of local coronation queens:
Wainfelin Coronation Queen was 10-year-old Judith Pert and picked to attend
her were Margaret Reardon, Penywain Street; Barbara Edwards, Campbell
Street; Jean Winstone, St. John's Crescent and Helen Simmonds, Fairfield.
Garndiffaith's Carnival Queen was pretty twelve-year-old Wendy George of 60,
Penylan Road, Varteg. Her selected court ladies were Kay Matthews of 22, Rock
Villa Close; Pauline Courtney, The Avenue, Garndiffaith; Elizabeth Mabbit, 2,
Bryn Terrace, Garndiffaith and Marie Smith, 7, Brightstown, Garndiffaith.

Blaenafon's Forge Side Queen was Marjorie Stokes a pretty 20 year old from 18, High Street, Abersychan.

A charming brunette, Joyce Matthews, of Cinder Pit Cottage, Blaenafon became Coronation Queen for the Blaenafon Hospital Fete and her juvenile court consisted of Ann Morris, Sandra White, Valerie Bollen, and Jacqueline Carver.

Talywain chose 18 years old Jean Williams as their adult Queen and court ladies Maureen Turley, Talywain; Jean Horler, Pentwyn; Betty Johnson, Talywain; Margaret Watson, Abersychan.

Twelve year old Valerie Bollen picked up the Talywain "Queen of the Roses" title with court ladies Jeanette Green, Ann Warenbury, Sandra Trumper, Diane Luter, and Pat Leaky.

Blue-eyed Christine Williams became a popular Queen at Cwnffrwdoer with Valerie Marsh, Jennifer Pooley, Jacqueline Morgan and Sylvia Smallcombe in attendance. Small children as ladies-in-waiting were Yvonne Morris, Julie Parry, Lynette Wells, and Rosaline Kerr.

Pretty 14-year-old Hazel Tovey, of Pontnewynydd, became a successful Queen for Freeholdland, Pontnewynydd.

Coronation Day for pretty Heather Romaine Phillips, aged 18 years, of 24 Bridge Street, Griffithstown, was extra special as it was her wedding day. While Queen Elizabeth was riding in the State Coach to Westminster Abbey, Heather was in a taxi bound for Griffithstown Methodist Chapel. There she married William John (Billy) Rodgers, who worked at the Royal Ordinance Factory and was the eldest son of Mr and Mrs John Rodgers, of Penygarn. His club captain, Jack Bryant, delivered Billy, well known as the Pontnewydd Rugby Club hooker, to the church. The issue of this union was a beautiful baby girl.

Two Torfaen men would receive the specially struck Coronation Medal. For his courage and endurance Clifford William Kendall, a 32 year-old injured ex-serviceman, from Woodside Road, Pontnewynydd, received his medal at Rookwood Hospital, a rehabilitation centre in Cardiff. For Pontypool's William John Smith, DSM, it would be his second Coronation medal, the first was from the late King George VI. Residing in Gwent Street, Pontypool, 73 year-old Mr. Smith won the Distinguished Service Medal as a gun layer in 1917 during action against an enemy submarine.

It had been a wonderful time and is still vivid in the memories of Torfaen folk. Only a few far-sighted people at that time suspected what a great contribution the new, young Queen would make to all our lives. Probably one of the few was the editor of the Free Press of Monmouthshire newspaper when he wrote the following front-page editorial for the June 5th 1953 issue:

Her Majesty's loyal subjects in this green, industrial Eastern Valley of Monmouthshire acclaimed the Coronation of Queen Elizabeth II with joy and affection surpassed nowhere in Britain or the Commonwealth.

In their homely, sincere and unpretentious way, the people of the valley have hailed the new Elizabethan Era amid scenes of spectacle, colour and gay festivity.

Not a man, woman or child has escaped the thrilling impact of these historic days. Not a street, shop or factory is without its flags and pictures of our beautiful Sovereign and her husband, the Duke of Edinburgh.

With every toast, song, dance and act of worship, the valley has re-pledged its faith both in the Crown and in those ideals of peace and progress of which it is the gleaming symbol.

Only three colours count in the valley this week – green has given way to red, white and blue, fluttering happily and proudly wherever people dwell.

For one and all, it is a time of jubilation and thanksgiving, of homage to the World's First Lady and of re-avowed unity among the nations over which she rules.

Born on Coronation Day, Mrs Gail (Parry) Flight, with her mother Betty Parry, of Blaenafon.

Chapter Six

THE ROYAL VISIT TO PONTYPOOL

P eople everywhere took the new Queen to their hearts. Coronation day proved to be only the beginning of a long and wonderful adventure for a young woman and her people. In Torfaen the excitement was far from over. It became known that the county of Gwent had been honoured with a visit in July to Newport and district, as the first stage of Her Majesty's post-coronation tour.

Thousands of parents and children, caught up in the wonder of this new reign, travelled down the eastern valley for the chance of getting a glimpse of their Queen. The word went around as to where the best observation spot would be on the Royal route. Organised trips for the children of Pentwyn Council School and Varteg Mixed were well attended, the teachers deciding to wait at Bassaleg for a good view of passing Royals. Torfaen was almost deserted because of the huge exodus. Bus queues had begun forming throughout the valley at an early hour and by 8 a.m., the entire fleet of buses attached to the Pontnewynydd depot of the Western Welsh Bus Company was in service. Panic had set in by this time at Cwmbran where three privately owned coaches failed to turn up to transport a large number of excited children. However, the Western Welsh Bus Company somehow found transport for the children. Every special train organised by British Railways was full to capacity. In the words of one elderly gentleman, "By midday it was like a Sunday in Pontypool."

Wherever they were waiting on the special route they would be warned of the arrival of the Royals at Newport Railway Station by the 21 gun salute, fired by the 56 Heavy Anti-Aircraft Regiment at Newport Barracks.

A huge cheer greeted Her Majesty as she walked out of Newport Railway Station to inspect the guard of honour. At one point she stopped to talk to Pontlottyn born Sergeant E.T. Chapman, who won the Victoria Cross in World War Two. A long time resident of Torfaen, Mr. Chapman would later remember the moment well.

Amid the cheers the Royal couple toured the area. "Good old Phillip" shouted one spectator and got a smile in acknowledgement. The children loved the experience of greeting their new Queen. At Newport Civic Centre the Queen paused before entering for the playing of the National Anthem. Immediately afterwards a faint blush flooded

71

her cheeks as the children, no longer able to contain their feelings, burst forth in the only unrehearsed song of the morning – *"Isn't she marvellous."*

It had been a memorable day in the lives of the people of Torfaen, and sometime before a similar, stirring event, would again be experienced.

It would be almost ten years to the day before the people of Torfaen had the opportunity to see their Sovereign again. The welcome news of her visit was first received in a meeting of the Pontypool Urban District Council on April 8th, 1963. The minute book recorded:

> *The Clerk reported that he had been informed that Her Majesty The Queen and His Royal Highness The Duke of Edinburgh would be calling at the Town Hall, Pontypool, during their visit to Monmouthshire on 10 May 1963.*
>
> *The Clerk informed the Council that Her Majesty and The Duke of Edinburgh were to visit Abergavenny and Cwrt-y-Gollen Camp, Crickhowell, during the morning of the 10th May 1963, and later in the day they were due at the British Nylon Factory. When the Queen and The Duke left the Cwrt-y-Gollen Camp they would travel via Crickhowell, Gilwern and the mountain road to Blaenavon Council Offices at about 2.55 p.m., and travel via Cwmavon, Abersychan and Pontnewynydd to arrive at the Town Hall, Pontypool, about 3.25 p.m., where they would meet the Chairman, Vice Chairman and Clerk of the County Council. The Queen and The Duke of Edinburgh would leave the Town Hall at approximately 3.35 p.m., to travel to the British Nylon Factory.*
>
> *The Clerk suggested that the Council should appoint a small Sub-Committee consisting of members who were readily available, with plenary powers, to deal with the arrangements of the Royal Visit.*
>
> <u>*Resolved*</u> *that the Sub-Committee consisting of the Chairman of the Council, the Vice-Chairman of the Council, Councillors E.H. Parker, G.R. Trim, J.P., W.L. Jackson and A.C. Jones, be set up with plenary powers, to make arrangements for the Queen's visit and any re-decoration that may be necessary.*

It was a miserable wet day when the Royal couple arrived at Abergavenny (Monmouth Road) Railway Station at 10.15 a.m. Yet, this did not deter the people of Abergavenny or any spectators during their busy day. Following a visit to the ancient parish church of St. Mary's, the Royal entourage headed for Cwrt-y-Gollen, Crickhowell. Here the Queen officially opened the new Headquarters of Welsh Brigade during a colourful military ceremony. The many relatives of staff had made the short journey from Abergavenny to see the proceeding and as always, 'Sospan' the goat of the 4th Battalion Welch Regiment (TA) enchanted the young visitors. After lunch in the officer's mess the Royal party left for Blaenafon.

Most parts of the long mountain road saw spectators braving the poor weather to obtain a good view of the party as it passed. The pupils and staff of Blaenafon Park Street Secondary School went to Cae White where they had an excellent viewpoint. A great ovation met the Queen as she entered the Blaenafon Council building escorted by Council Chairman Miss May Lewis. Here, the Royal couple signed the visitor's book and Royal photographs. Its owner, Mr. Fred Percy, later presented an attractive Victorian inkstand loaned during the hurried preparations, and used during the visit, to the Council as a keepsake. Although running late, the Queen appeared with Miss Lewis on the building's balcony and waved to the cheering crowd for several minutes. Those presented to the Queen in the short time allowed were: Mr. Noel Lewis, Mr. J. Protheroe, clerk and chief financial officer, Councillors S. Banks, vice chairman, W.H. Arnold, G. Bailey, T. Bond, E.J. Davies, C. Evans, A.P. Griffiths, E.J. Hobbs, K. Keen, R.J. Morris, W.H. Parry, J.C. Peters, D.W. Puddle, A.R. Targett, W.H. Taylor, and R.A. Watkins.

The Queen and Council Chairman Miss May Lewis
on the balcony of the Municipal Offices, Blaenafon

The Royal procession passed through Cwmavon, Abersychan and Pontnewynydd to reach the outskirts of Pontypool. In a short time, and the same as everywhere else, the district had been spruced up. The Council had wisely decided that the people of the Pontypool Urban District were entitled to have something special to remember for the remainder of their lives, particularly the children. Much of the work had been a voluntary undertaking, and what little money the Council spent was for badly needed improvements about to be commenced before the visit was known. Bunting and flags were everywhere. As the Queen's maroon-coloured, glass topped, Rolls Royce came into view a loud roar echoed through the valley town. Immediately in front of the large crowd outside the Town Hall were members of the Pontypool unit of sea cadets (TS Kittiwake), and representatives of the boy scouts and girl guides.

The same time as the Queen's car came to a halt outside the Pontypool Town Hall a man stepped forward that appeared to have been born for this special moment in Torfaen history. The tall, handsome man had all the attributes of one who might have mixed with nobles every day of his life. He was the chairman of the Pontypool Urban Council, Mr. Cyril Irving, accompanied by his attractive wife. As the Queen stepped out of the car her first words to Councillor Irving was, "What a wonderful crowd." Six old soldiers representing the British Legion branches in the Pontypool area stood to attention in the town hall corridor as the Royal visitors passed. They were Messrs. G.E. Allen and G. C. Preece (Panteg), A.Haynes and W. Taylor (Pontnewynydd), and R. Burchall and E. Shears (Pontypool). Upstairs, in the recently decorated Assembly Room, the Queen took tremendous interest in the collection of Japan Ware, rare specimens of Pontypool's old industry. Presented to the Queen on the memorable day in the Town Hall were: Vice-chairman Councillor Mrs F.M. Prosser, Mr. H. Cook, clerk, Councillors N. Townsend, W. Higgs, W.C. Chivers, J.D.C. Webster, E.H. Parker, S.W. Ball, N.L. Hillman, G. Trim, H.J. Rosser, Mrs E.M. Hill, W.G. Hillier, J.H. Evans, Mrs M.L. Lee, A.C. Jones, J.R. Kilminster, R.E. Moore, H. Bullimore, and Mrs A.M. Moore. Before leaving the Town Hall the Queen and Duke were invited to sign the visitor's book and autograph several large photographs.

The last call in a long day for the Royal couple was to the British Nylon Spinners factory on the outskirts of Pontypool. The Duke's interest in all the new technology on show would cause the Queen to often turn around and enquire where he was. On display at the factory were nylon gifts for the Royal family. Nylon anoraks for the Queen, Princess Anne, Prince Charles and Prince Andrew, created a great deal of interest, while the Duke received a nylon spinnaker for his yacht Bloodhound.

It was time to leave the old district of Torfaen and hundreds cheered farewell at Pontypool Road Station as the party arrived at the waiting Royal train. Rarely does a small town or village have the honour of witnessing a great monarch in their midst and May 10 1963, was a day that local folk would never forget.

QUEEN'S VISIT TO PONTYPOOL, IN 1963.

Queen Elizabeth admires Pontypool Japanware.

Chapter Seven

THE SILVER JUBILEE of 1977

Due to frightening unemployment figures in Torfaen, 1977 would be one of the bleakest years on record. It seemed that every industry in the valley was hit by redundancies and many older members of the community began to recall former dark days of industrial depression. However, there was a silver lining to the miserable year. In June, Her Majesty Queen Elizabeth II had reigned a remarkable twenty-five years.

Plans were underway for Her Majesty to again use the famous gold Coronation Coach during her Silver Jubilee procession, and the early release of her huge programme for the year showed a tour of South Wales on June 24th. The popular tour was to be similar to that of Coronation year and again ended in Cardiff. Souvenirs of all descriptions began to appear and made folk more interested in the forthcoming celebration. The coveted Silver Jubilee souvenir became a commemorative silver medal struck and to be issued as a personal award from Her Majesty to members of the Crown services, and others in the United Kingdom and Commonwealth countries. Many parents would buy each of their children a commemorative crown piece issued by the Royal Mint, and with a face value of 25p. For stamp collectors, obtaining four colourful sets of Jubilee stamps was a must followed by a visit to the large stamp exhibition organised by the Post Office in City Hall, Cardiff. The traditional Jubilee appeal got underway with the help of the heir to the throne. On this occasion the aim of the Silver Jubilee Fund – at the Queen's express wish – was to help young people to make a contribution to the communities in which they lived.

The year started well for Blaenafon resident Llewellyn C. Browning, he was awarded the MBE in the New Years' Honours List. He served with the Blaenafon Iron and Coal Company for many years and also had the distinction of being the great-grandson of Lewis Browning, a former miner, who wrote one of the first histories of Blaenafon in 1906.

Thoughts turned to the summer celebration and the never-to-be lost community spirit in Torfaen appeared once more like the Phoenix rising out of the ashes. Although consisting of only ten houses in the road, Ashgrove Road, Trevethin, set a determined example for all to follow. Collections had begun the previous year and already forty mugs had been purchased for the children and twenty-five plaques for the adults. With thoroughfares more busy it became a sensible step to seek permission from the Council to hold a party in a particular street or road. To heighten interest further, and add to the fun of the celebrations, the Torfaen Borough Council boosted the Silver Jubilee festivities by bringing forward the town's annual carnival week.

When asked to consider being Mayor for 1977, Sebastopol born Graham Powell had not realised that his year as Torfaen's first citizen coincided with the great occasion of the Silver Jubilee of his Sovereign. Again, Torfaen was fortunate to have a man who would rise to the special occasion. Commencing his new duty in May, he and his wife Daisy, would do everything possible to promote the good name of Torfaen. One of his first tasks following his installation was to send loyal greetings to the Queen on behalf of the citizens of the borough. The text of his letter is as follows:

With my humble duty, on my first day as Mayor of the Borough of Torfaen, I extend loyal greetings from Council members and citizens in this great Silver Jubilee Year.

We are certain it will be as memorable for us as it will be for Your Majesty, and, it gave me great pleasure to launch today a public appeal fund in support of the Silver Jubilee Appeal Committee for Gwent.

The aim is to set up a training centre for youth leaders in suitably adapted countryside premises, which are being sought in the county. It is a most worthwhile project of the kind, which we know, is very dear to Your Majesty's heart, and I am sure that Torfaen will contribute generously.

In readiness for the celebrations, Merle Everett was chosen as carnival Jubilee Queen for both Blaenafon and Pontypool. Her court ladies at Pontypool consisted of four attractive young ladies: Kerry Thorpe, Gail Thomas, Amanda Chambers and Cheryl Stone. The junior Rose Queen for the Pontypool Jubilee Carnival became Diana Williams, a pretty thirteen year old, of Hospital Road, Pontnewynydd.

At the Congress Theatre, the result of the Cwmbran Jubilee Queen contest would be a dramatic affair. Diana Jenkins, of St Dials, only turned up to watch the proceedings, but was persuaded to enter the contest. In a dress loaned by Merle Everett, she won her first ever beauty contest. Chosen as her court attendants were Lyn Stanley, of Greenmeadow and Gail Thomas, of Croesyceiliog. Out of sixty entries the Rose Queen title went to eleven-year-old Chantelle Morgan, of Blaendare, Pontypool.

The unique spectacle in London, on Silver Jubilee Day, was admired all around the world. A number of Torfaen men would be on duty along the route of the prodigious procession to the Thanksgiving Service in St. Paul's Cathedral. The dedicated members of the St. John's Ambulance Brigade were Mr. S. Morgan, Mr. I. Morgan, Mr. W. Galloway, Blaenafon Division, and Mr. G. Jones, Mr. B. Long and Mr. D. Gordon, of the Cwmbran Division.

Merle Everett Pontypool and Blaenafon Silver Jubilee Queen, 1977.

*Crowning of Cwmbran's
Silver Jubilee Queen, 1977.
Diane Jenkins of St. Dials,
Cwmbran.*

*Cwmbran's 1977 Silver
Jubilee "Rose Queen"
Chantelle Morgan, 11 years.*

Diane Jenkins, Cwmbran's Silver Jubilee Queen, 1977.

In Torfaen it was a wonderful time with people enjoying street parties and entertainment organised by the Torfaen Borough Council. The Mayor had a busy time on Jubilee Day visiting street parties throughout Torfaen. His message of best wishes to the Queen brought a letter from Buckingham Palace signed by one of the royal secretaries:

I am commanded by the Queen to thank you for your letter of May 26, and for the kind message of loyal greetings, which you sent on behalf of the Council members and citizens of the Borough of Torfaen.

Her Majesty thought the project, in aid of which you have launched your public appeal, a most worthwhile one and has instructed me to send her very best wishes for the successful achievement of your objective.

The special day of June 7th would produce an overwhelming event at Panteg Hospital, Griffithstown. Here, Torfaen's only Jubilee baby arrived. A beautiful daughter was born to Margaret Gulliford, of West End Avenue, Pontnewydd.

Torfaen would be blessed with a good haul of the specially struck Silver Jubilee Medals issued as a personal award from Her Majesty. The recipients were:

> Mr. I.A. Jenkins, Twyn-y-Ffrwd, Abersychan
> Mr. J.F. Jobbins, New Inn
> Miss Megan Jones, Pontnewynydd
> Mr. Ronald Porcher, Llanyravon
> Mr. Owen Waters, Pentwyn
> Mr. Bernard Skinner, Griffithstown
> Mr. William F. Hall, Sebastopol
> Mr. M.B. Mehta, Griffithstown
> Mr. Frederick Gifford, Cwmbran
> Mr. Dennis Puddle, Blaenafon

Further medals were awarded to Torfaen residents in the Queens Birthday Honours list: Mr. Arthur Dunning, of Charston, Greenmeadow, Cwmbran, received the British Empire Medal for exemplary service to the Ministry of Defence; and Mr. Digby Rees, of Wainfelin Avenue, Pontypool, also received the British Empire Medal for his work at the Royal Ordnance Factory, Glascoed.

It had been another wonderful royal occasion in Torfaen, thanks to the hard work put in by representatives of the Council and the huge band of enthusiastic volunteers. For a while the gloom was lifted and folk forgot the harsh reality of everyday living.

Without doubt, the special relationship between Queen Elizabeth II and the citizens of the Borough of Torfaen will always endure. There could be no more proof of this than to have heard the voices, raised in joyous song, at the Mayor's Thanksgiving Service in Pontypool, which, for a while, would bring the magical time to an end.

Mr. Arthur Dunning, of Greenmeadow, Cwmbran, receives British Empire Medal.

The Mayor of Torfaen, Councillor Graham Powell, hands a £5 note to Borough Treasurer, Mr. Ernest Keeley, to start the Silver Jubilee Appeal Fund.

Replica Crown Jewels on show at Pontypool Jubilee Carnival and Ideal Home Exhibition, 1977.

Court Farm, Llantarnam, Silver Jubilee Queen,
L.R. Valerie Cook, Destra James, Sian Rees.

Tynes, Coed Eva, Cwmbran, Silver Jubilee Party.

Two Locks, Cwmbran Silver Jubilee Party.

West Rodin, Coed Eva, Cwmbran, Silver Jubilee Party.

Street party, Pontrhydyrun.

Samantha Hall and Neil Jones at Pontrhydyrun Street Party.

New Inn Silver Jubilee Party.

Greenway, Griffithstown, Silver Jubilee Party, M.B. Mehta, Graham Powell, George Scrivens.

Silver Jubilee Party at Heol Deinol, New Inn.

New Inn Street Party

Princess Walk, New Inn Silver Jubilee Party.

New Inn Jubilee Street Party.
Left to right: Samantha Williams, Clair Watkins, Johnathan Williams, Louis Jobbins.

Ashgrove Close, Trevethin Silver Jubilee Street Party.

More fun at Ashgrove Close, Trevethin Street Party.

Future council workers at Ashgrove Close, Trevethin 1977 Silver Jubilee Party.

Silver Jubilee Day at Charlesville, Pontnewynydd.

1977 - 10 year old Emma Davies of Holyoak Terrace, Pontnewynydd.

Silver Jubilee Party at Llanover Road, Blaenafon.

Chapter Eight

LONG MAY SHE REIGN

T he time has arrived to celebrate Her Majesty's fifty years on the Throne and her contribution to life in the United Kingdom and throughout the Commonwealth. When asked about the plans for the special year in the House of Commons Prime Minister Blair stated:

"I am pleased to be able to announce that Her Majesty The Queen has approved a number of recommendations for the programme of celebrations during 2002, the focal point of which will be the 'Jubilee weekend' period covering 1 to 4 June. As I announced on 23 November 2000, Tuesday 4 June will be a Bank Holiday in place of the Spring Bank Holiday that would otherwise fall on 27 May 2002, and Monday 3 June will be an additional Bank Holiday for the Golden Jubilee...This significant national anniversary of fifty years of The Queen's reign will offer people of all ages and cultures and from all walks of life the opportunity for celebration, and the events surrounding the Jubilee will provide numerous opportunities for voluntary and community service. It should be a time for looking forward as well as back at the great changes that have taken place in the nation's life during Her Majesties reign."

Following these announcements, and with the huge strides made improving communications during recent years, the early awareness of the general public to such a great event as the Golden Jubilee of Queen Elizabeth II became a certainty. Her Majesties official Golden Jubilee Website made known six themes to deliver the celebrations:

1. CELEBRATION
The Queen has expressed the wish that her Golden Jubilee should be an occasion for celebration involving the whole community in this country and throughout the Commonwealth. The focal point of the celebrations will be the National Service of Thanksgiving at St Paul's Cathedral on Tuesday 4 June 2002 on the final day of a Jubilee weekend of special events to mark the Golden Jubilee starting on Saturday 1 June. The summer of 2002, from May to July, will be given over to celebrations in every city, region, county, town and village across the United Kingdom.

2. GIVING THANKS

The Queen has said that she sees her Golden Jubilee as an opportunity to express her thanks for the support and loyalty she has enjoyed during her reign. This is to be a central theme of the Golden Jubilee celebrations. Through Her Majesty's visits around the United Kingdom and overseas during 2002 there will be many opportunities to pay tribute to all those who have supported the Queen over the last fifty years. Her Majesty's tours will also provide citizens of this country and the Commonwealth nation with opportunities to thank her for fifty years dedicated service.

3. SERVICE

The Golden Jubilee celebrations will provide a special opportunity to acknowledge all those who support and contribute to their communities through public service and voluntary endeavour.

4. INVOLVING THE WHOLE COMMUNITY

The Queen hopes that the celebrations will reach into every community and involve everyone no matter what their background, age, culture, ethnic origin, religion or other status. It is hoped that the Golden Jubilee will be an inclusive occasion; that the celebrations will be accessible to all those who want to participate; and that they will reflect the multiculturalism in our society today and the diversity we see around us.

5. LOOKING FORWARD AS WELL AS BACK

The celebration of a 50-year reign is a time for reflection on the ways in which our lives have changed over half a century. It also offers us the chance to take stock of where we stand today and to look to the future. The Golden Jubilee is as much for young people in our communities as it is for the older generation. Celebrating the achievements of the youth of the United Kingdom and the Commonwealth and looking ahead to the contribution of youth to our society are important aspects of the Golden Jubilee.

6. COMMONWEALTH

The significance of the Commonwealth to the development and modern life of our nation is central to the programme of Golden Jubilee events scheduled for 2002. There is an important Commonwealth dimension to each of the other themes, which places the Commonwealth at the heart of the Jubilee.

Some facts have emerged which gives just a little indication of the tremendous workload our Sovereign undertook during the past fifty years:

Signed 3,000 Acts of Parliament.
Completed over 250 overseas tours.
Given eighty-eight State banquets.
Launched seventeen ships
Over 1,000,000 people attended Her garden parties.
38,630 honours presented to the famous and not so famous.
Received 3,000,000 letters.
100,000 telegrams sent to centenarians.
Sat for 120 portraits.

The Golden Jubilee year 2002 commenced well in London with a New Year Parade. More than 30,000 people lined the streets to see 6,000 entertainers in colourful costumes giving a display of their remarkable talents. The Queen sent a message: "I hope that 2002 will prove to be one of fulfilment to everyone, and that today's parade will launch the year in suitable style." A sneak preview of the Queen's new car for

Jubilee year also created interest. The custom built Bentley, to be used for state occasions, and handed over in May, is a suitable gift for Her Majesty's Golden Jubilee. Both the Queen and the Duke of Edinburgh were closely involved in its design. Closer to home, the people of Torfaen only have to travel across the Severn Bridge to Bath to see a unique collection of the Queen's original clothes at the Costume Museum.

Many wish to be among the first to own a remarkable new Royal Mint memento. The new £5 Golden Jubilee Crown, struck to a brilliant uncirculated standard, and obtained in a presentation folder costing £9.95, is set to break all sales records at the Royal Mint gift shop in Llantrisant, near Pontypridd.

Believed to be a bonus for the special year, the Commonwealth Games will commence in Manchester on July 25, and are to be opened by Her Majesty. As a supplement to the important athletic event, a Golden Jubilee baton relay sets off on March 11 and travels around the country until the start of the games. Around 5,000 athletes, celebrities and disabled people will carry the baton containing the Queen's message.

The extended bank holiday weekend from 1 to 4 June 2002, will allow the whole country to celebrate the 50-year reign and to have a good time. In London the events planned for the Jubilee Weekend are:

Saturday 1 June   Classical concert in Buckingham Palace Garden.

Sunday 2 June   Jubilee Church services and bell ringing across the country.

Monday 3 June   Pop concert in Buckingham Palace Garden reflecting popular songs of the past fifty years; followed by beacon lighting and firework display.

Tuesday 4 June   Ceremonial procession to St. Paul's Cathedral for the National Service of Thanksgiving. Lord Mayor of London hosts lunch at the Guildhall. In the afternoon the Golden Jubilee Carnival Pageant in the Mall.

It was a splendid start to the special year in Torfaen when the news arrived that a popular local councillor had received a well-deserved Member of the British Empire award. Councillor Ivor Davies has served the Snatchwood, Abersychan community since 1974; turning out in all weathers and times to solve immediate problems. A retired Ambulance Service worker, and a true man of the valley, he receives his award for tireless community work. An MBE award also went to the welfare officer of the Gwent Constabulary. Mr. Nigel Graham Pocknell, of Cwmbran, received his well-earned award for services to retired police officers. Prince Charles will make the presentations at Cardiff Castle.

Golden Jubilee Year sees the conclusion of the term of office of Cwmbran Councillor Colette Thomas as Mayor of Torfaen. It has been an excellent year for Councillor Thomas who has worked non-stop promoting the good name of the area. Besides the dedication and hard work during her twelve-month tenure, she has portrayed a rare dignity in all things. This has been truly appreciated by the people of Torfaen. It will be a busy year for Councillor J.J. (Jack) Everson, who takes over the reins and will be Mayor of Torfaen during the Golden Jubilee celebrations. With the total support of his wife Mavis he has served the Brynwern district of Pontypool for

Cllr. Ivor Davies, MBE.   *Mr. Nigel G. Pocknell, MBE.*

Cllr. J.J. Everson,
Mayor of Torfaen,
2002.

the past twelve years. No one can doubt his commitment to enhancing the quality of life in Torfaen. This was witnessed in 1994, when, as a master mason by trade, he rebuilt most of the Folly Tower with his bare hands.

In Torfaen it is not the objective to equal or excel other great events in the past, but for everyone to enjoy the Royal occasion, particularly the children. With the children in mind, the exciting preparations are underway. For them it is not only the opportunity to enjoy a rare occasion, but also to participate and learn from the many events taking place everywhere.

As on so many successful occasions before, the main Golden Jubilee events will be held in Pontypool Park. With the arrival of Alex Andrews as manager, the park has been beautifully restored to its former glory in time for the great occasion. Over the Jubilee weekend, once more the old and venerate park will echo with the joyous cries of delight of the young as they join in the purposeful entertainments. With street and garden parties everywhere, and senior citizens thoroughly spoiled, the ever-present community spirit will no doubt prevail; and, in all probability, the spirit of Gus Bevan, the man who raised little Pontypool from obscurity in 1887, will shine through and again touch the proud and noble people of Torfaen.